What People
The Art of Forgiveness

"The *Art of Forgiveness* is a clear, fun, and powerful book. CJ Jones uses her personal story of transformation to illustrate her *YIPPEE Method* of changing resentment into empowerment, and simultaneously shares expertise in the psychology and spirituality of forgiveness. Reading this book helped me develop my existing forgiveness skills to a much higher level and finally release the negative emotions that had bothered me for many years."
~ *Ivan Galperin, Student*

"Your entire book has been a healing process for me. It has helped me gain insight into my stuff. These are things I've worked on 30+ years that I've now resolved."
~ *C. Ana York, Reader*

"This book is a comprehensive guide that leads you past resentments that may be preventing you from having peace. Carolyn CJ Jones explores the pain these resentments play in your life, then uses her *YIPPEE Method* as a guide to get past them so you can discover peace. I found her story compelling and hard to put down! I recommend *The Art of Forgiveness* as a tool to find peace and freedom in your life."
~ *Pattie Meizis, Entrepreneur*

"CJ makes it clear how much time, energy, and even our well-being, are sacrificed to holding resentments. Her suggestion to write with our non-dominant hand is a great exercise to broaden our perspective. The technique she has developed to help us forgive others, as well as ourselves, can truly bring peace."
~ *Becky, Personal Wellness Consultant*

"It is the stories CJ shares in the *Art of Forgiveness* that reveal her humanity. In this sharing, she grants you permission to explore your *own* humanity without shame or humiliation, but rather, with curiosity. As a retired psychotherapist of forty years and a current wellness business coach, I found in CJ's book an approach that facilitates healing from wounds that lead to anger and resentment. Hers is a gentle and compassionate approach to deal with these feelings that may be consuming your life. In the process of exploring, you discover forgiveness and this leads you to great peace and freedom."
~ *Iris Stallworth-Grayling, LMFT (Ret), Wellness Business Coach*

THE ART

of

FORGIVENESS

A Promise of Peace

Carolyn CJ Jones

Dedications

"Once in a while, we are given moments of real grace."
Oriah Mountain Dreamer, *The Invitation*

I'd like to dedicate this book…

To each of you struggling with anger and resentment.
May moments of grace find you.

To Brad,
For your kindness.

To my roommate in early sobriety,
For being there with compassion and love.

To my spiritual advisor in recovery,
For furthering my ability to live sober, with Spirit.

To the thousands of men and women in the rooms,
For your kind ears and hearts.

To friends and colleagues,
For sharing your hearts and wisdom.

To my parents and siblings,
For your steadfast love and support
Throughout the highs and lows of my journey.

With my deepest thank you and gratitude, cj

Table of Contents

Acknowledgments

No book is created in a writer's vacuum. This one is no exception. It is a delight for me to recognize you who made this book possible, from its inception through to the reality of a finished product.

For all who read it, engaged in debate about the book's points, suggested edits, provided input on the cover, and offered support to me, you made the book stronger and more beautiful. Thank you!

C. Ana York, Shelley Dorssers, Rebecca Jones, Annie Oden, Berta Bollinger, Akikta Murti, Sumaya O'Grady, Pattie Meizis, Jim Dincalci, Jeanne Alford, and Pam Lunstead

For book and cover design, Cris Wanzer. Thank you for your wizardry. I love both!

For the New York cover design consultants. Your input was invaluable. Fun, fabulous processing!

Rebecca Jones, Mary Jane Auns, Sandy Turner, Philippa Weismann, and Mindy Lakin

For Dr. Jim Dincalci, C. Ana York, and Maura McCarley Torkildson, for your kind, thoughtful, and powerful portrayals of the book. I am proud they are on the cover!

For Dr. Fred Luskin, for your generous and gracious foreword. I am honored it precedes my story.

I'd like to especially acknowledge the following authors for their permission to quote passages and ideas from their books or articles. Thank you.

Dr. Fred Luskin, Ph.D., *Forgive for Good: A PROVEN Prescription for Health and Happiness*

Ms. Mary Beth Sammons and Ms. Nina Lesowitz, *Living Life as a Thank You: The Transformative Power of Daily Gratitude*

Ms. Robin Casarjian, M.A., *Houses of Healing: A Prisoner's Guide to Inner Power and Freedom*

Dr. Jim Dincalci, *How to Forgive When You Can't: The Breakthrough Guide to Free Your Heart and Mind*

Ms. Maura McCarley Torkildson, M.A., *Tackling Trauma*

National Institute for the Clinical Application of Behavioral Medicine

Dr. Sandra Wilson, Ph.D., *Hurt People Hurt People: Hope and Healing for Yourself and Your Relationships*

Dr. Bernard Golden, Ph.D., *Overcoming Destructive Anger: Strategies That Work*

Ms. Oriah Mountain Dreamer, *The Invitation*

Foreword

I am a professional psychologist and a researcher from Stanford University. I study and teach people the value of and how to teach forgiveness. My work comes from my head, powers of observation, from data, and mostly from the suffering of others. *The Art of Forgiveness* describes a journey and education that comes from CJ's soul. She suffered for her understanding and her wisdom is forged from courage, tenacity, and a ruthless honesty about herself. What is encouraging to me is we both end up at a pretty similar place – namely, the necessity of learning forgiveness to heal oneself and the world.

This book is raw. It does not spare us the pain she experienced nor the growth she accomplished. She forges a link between pain and anger and its resolution into forgiveness that is compelling. Her *YIPPEE Method* is a roadmap out of resentment into freedom and forgiveness. Her honesty extends to telling of the people and books that helped her along the way. In this book, CJ empties herself to share her experiences and learning for our benefit. You can feel her generosity of offering.

I particularly resonate with a couple of key points that she makes. First is the essential nature of gratitude in the process of forgiveness. At this point, I understand that we can take any life experience and hold it with either gratitude or complaint. Both of us have found gratitude to be the opposite of complaint and the grease of forgiveness. Second, I appreciate her radical honesty. She does not want to deceive herself any longer. And, with the link to gratitude, it turns out when we tell the truth, life offers us wonderful experiences and opportunities.

I have taught forgiveness throughout this world for hurts big and small. I believe I can recognize another person who understands the immense importance of forgiveness and who has created reliable methods to create it. Such a person has written the book you are about to read.

Frederic Luskin, Ph.D.

Preface

This book came to be reality in a most roundabout way... An email showed up in my inbox one day, alerting me of a writing contest. The winner was required to write a book. It piqued my interest, as the thought of writing one about forgiveness had been percolating in my heart and mind. The email also grabbed my attention because I have been writing essays and submitting them to contests. This was one more I could enter. Additionally, as a contributor to the *Unlimited Woman Magazine*, I thought that experience could be helpful for me in my writing for this specific contest. Based on these considerations, I decided to enter. On Christmas Day, I submitted my application.

Each contestant was required to email three documents. One document, the essay response, was to include an answer to a question the contest had posed. Within the framework of that question, it was necessary to describe a book the contestant proposed to write. The single winner will be required to write the book he/she discussed in his/her entry essay response.

In the course of answering the contest's question, I proposed to share my story to make the point it is possible to grow beyond anger and resentment to a place of peace and freedom using forgiveness. I specifically referenced mass shooters who are in need of healing the wounds underneath their anger. In my experience, my own long-standing anger and resentment were transformed to peace and freedom. Actually, it was through this personal experience that I learned how to transcend and rise above my anger and bitterness over the past. I was a victim for thirty of my adult years. To cope, I drank and drugged over it all. Today, I am a woman who lives in gratitude and positivity - at peace, free from resentment - all because I got sober, forgave, and found gratitude.

I've lived in both worlds. I can say with utter certainty that peace and freedom is the better of the two. It is well worth facing any obstacles you may experience as you work through the healing process. The change from anger and resentment to gratitude and positivity is exquisite. I offer my story in order to share a map to navigate beyond any anger or resentment *you* may be harboring. Also, I write this book for you as a way to offer hope. HOPE is an acronym: Hold On, Pain Ends. It truly does. It also stands for Hold On, Possibilities Emerge. They do, thus, bringing delight into your life. These can both be true for you.

In addition to answering the question they posed, the contest required the essay to be timely and relevant. It was expected the author would back up with research any ideas and thoughts they proposed to put in the book. The topic I broached and discussed involved the feelings under anger and resentment. I talked about violence in the world, focusing on mass shootings. The shooters behind these tragedies are, in my estimation and per research, showing signs of deep anger and resentment. I contend these feelings can heal.

To offer clarity, let me relay my proposal for the contest was to write the book, *Forgive for the Sake of Humanity*. The essence of the essay was, it is possible to heal and grow beyond your anger and resentment. I mentioned gun violence and shootings that are out of control in our country and the world. Shooters act out their anger and resentment when they kill. However, the feelings underneath the anger are not examined, wounds are not healed. Perhaps, they could be helped with this. My book explores wounds and offers a way to heal them through forgiveness, thus, allowing the person exploring the wounds to gain peace and freedom. Having said this, and after submitting everything, I settled back to await the announcement of the winner, due in late May 2019. I continued my job as a senior caregiver.

In mid-February 2019, I lost that caregiving position without much warning. My client was moved from her home to a nursing facility; she was becoming unsafe alone. She loves it there and I'm relieved she does. Meanwhile, the bulk of my income disappeared. However, the family gave me a severance that would tide me over for a little bit. Then, an opportunity presented itself and I decided to act on it.

I saw this new situation as a possibility emerging, an opportunity knocking. I also saw it as a sign from Spirit to write my book. I decided to write it when the opportunity to show it at a large international book show presented itself. As winning the contest was certainly not guaranteed, I elected to write the book now, before I hear in May whether or not I am the winner. In the interim, after discussion with others, I elected to use some of my severance monies to gain entry into the show. My goal and intention in doing so is to generate interest in my book. The book's availability can be useful to anyone struggling with anger and resentment.

My intention in writing is to create a safe and trusting space in which you can rest and catch your breath. It is my sincere hope you are able to do this. If my story resonates with you and helps you forgive yourself and others, please freely use in your life what I have learned in mine.

Thank you in advance for your time and attention to the journey I lovingly present to you. As you read through the book, do not despair over my experiences, for my life evolved into great healings and gratitudes. Rather, celebrate the difficulties with me, as they have provided me a beautiful and fulfilling life. In like fashion, trust that as *you* use the information contained in these pages, you, too, can one day celebrate the beauty you have found in yourself and *your* life.

Blessings, cj

Carolyn CJ Jones
San Francisco Bay Area
May 2019

Introduction

My deepest desire in sharing this book is to be useful to those of you who are tired of anger or resentment affecting your life. Maybe it's impacting you negatively in some way or is causing difficulties. Through this writing, my wish for you is that any struggles you may be experiencing are eased. My goal is to minimize and, hopefully, resolve your emotional pain, so as to remove any need on your part to act out against someone else or inward against yourself. This writing is also an attempt to reach you if you're considering shooting someone over an argument. May these pages soothe you.

Finally, I wish to present words that evoke feelings within you such that you begin to *yearn* to join in the journey of forgiveness. In this way, you allow more peace and freedom into your life and the lives of those you love. I present you with thoughts, words, ideas, stories, and research that allow you to get beyond anger and resentment. These all work together so you gain the ability to transform relationships with others and yourself.

My focus in these pages is on the *process* of forgiveness. In my experience, forgiveness starts with willingness to consider forgiving someone; this includes forgiving yourself. Willingness is the key. It is needed for each successive stage. Using willingness, you move through six stages before forgiveness is realized. I call the entire process, including all the stages, the "art of forgiveness." This piece of "artwork" includes many different facets of information and mindset, all of which are needed to forgive. Within the art of forgiveness lies the *YIPPEE Method* you utilize to guide yourself through the stages. It demonstrates how to use curiosity and a yearning for peace and freedom to your advantage. You discover when you forgive, there is no room left for anger in your heart, in your soul.

The Art of Forgiveness: A Promise of Peace allows you to see from a new perspective, with fresh eyes. I share my stories as examples of ways to heal the hurt underneath any anger you may be feeling. Former clients say my tales contain pearls of wisdom and golden nuggets. I'll let you be the judge of that. These bits of wisdom were uncovered through difficult, yet, always growth-producing experiences. In sharing them, I provide you hope and the knowledge you're not alone. I offer you encouragement and support to know you can go through the process I share in this book.

Before continuing, let's define and take a look at anger and resentment. There is a distinction between them, as defined in Wikipedia. Resentment is anger felt over and over again, often accompanied with a desire for revenge. Anger, while it can be an appropriate response to danger, is defined as 1) a form of intense emotional response, and 2) antagonism toward someone, something, or yourself, usually combined with an urge to harm.

It bears mentioning that all anger is not toxic. It can be a reaction to injustice or harm being committed. If channeled well and appropriately, anger can be a powerful motivator for change.

Resentment, also called bitterness, is said to be recreated each time you think of an incident over which you are angry. Therefore, it goes around and around in your head as you experience the offense again and again. Spite is often a desire of resentful people. Resentment against yourself is known as remorse. I specify both anger and resentment when I refer to them, as opposed to using the terms interchangeably. I also occasionally insert the term grievance to encompass both.

It is my hope you who are hurting underneath anger, underneath resentment, will discover and read this book. It can guide you to the peace and freedom that exists beyond any angry and resentful feelings. If you participate in the writing exercises I offer to you throughout the book, you reach that space with more ease and grace.

When you embark upon the journey, I invite you to believe a spirit is guiding you, however you define and name that force. Trust in it. Watch for possibilities to emerge, for opportunities to present themselves. Allow yourself to grow and evolve each time you encounter an experience.

This book is coming to me through Spirit that shows up in my life as the calm, quiet voice in my head. I feel in my heart it is my guide and recognize it as my higher Self. When Spirit speaks to me in that soft, unruffled tone, I quiet myself and listen. The key is to recognize its voice, trust it, and then follow through with what it offers for me. My humble belief is that Spirit is guiding me to share with you how I got beyond my anger and resentment when I healed my wounds, so you can do the same. After all, the opportunity to go to the book show appeared out of nowhere. I was able to act upon it only because I'd lost my full time job and received severance monies. It was then I had the time to write and money to cover me for a short period. These were not accidents or coincidences.

What I discovered and gained on my own journey are the peace and freedom I believe many of you seek in your lives as well. The Dalai Lama advises, "We can never obtain peace in the outer world until we make peace with ourselves." Given that I have learned this to be true, I am compelled to write about *why* what he says is truth, and how to gain that inner peace he references. I know, for example, if feelings under anger are explored and forgiveness is achieved, anger is resolved. It cannot exist in the same space as the feelings such as gratitude and compassion needed to create forgiveness.

This book tells my story from deep despair to great joy. It follows the same course I took on my journey in recovery. Because of this, some chapters may seem out of place. For example, it was only after I discovered how to be grateful for *everything* that I was able to deal with my anger. I dealt with my angry feelings later in sobriety after healing had begun, after I had forgiven my past and discovered gratitude. Therefore, the *Anger, Resentment, and Beyond* chapter appears after the chapters, *The Art of Forgiveness* and the *YIPPEE Method* that are the healing chapters.

The level of anger and resentment people carry is disturbing to me. I am alarmed by all the hate, judgment, and negativity. These destructive feelings are running rampant in our society and literally *killing* people. Why, all of us are at risk of involvement in a random or mass shooting. Knowing this has created fear among us, sometimes panic. Thinking it could happen to you is alarming! For my part, I have the desire to act instead of blaming, wringing my hands, or living in fear. These killings speak to me as something with which we need to deal - now. We need to address the hurt, humiliated, or shamed feelings. They exist underneath the anger and resentment that prompt someone to pick up a gun and commit a mass shooting, or any shooting.

The things I experienced on my healing journey drastically changed who I was and am as a person. I began to wonder if the gunmen in mass shootings, or any shooting, could resolve *their* anger if they applied the technique I created. Perhaps if this occurred, we could stop the shootings. In other words, could what I learned be of use to them? Could the process I developed, the art of forgiveness, help heal shooters and prevent killings? I think if they read the book, it might.

I write and offer potentially helpful information that speaks to the shooters' issues, yet, this in no way detracts from my attention to you, the one who doesn't act out in violence when angry or resentful. What I present here is a compilation of thoughts, feelings, ideas, and solutions to these emotions experienced in the life of a human being.

Research shows that under anger, beneath resentment, are feelings such as hurt, disappointment, humiliation, and shame, frosted with that anger and resentment. People do not easily identify these feelings, let alone express them. Instead, they act out against someone in anger, perhaps looking for revenge. Or, they turn their resentment inward, creating remorse, sometimes harming themselves. It is because I see so many unhappy and angry people, and in consideration of the shooters, I feel the need to share my story.

Addressing the feelings under anger and resentment is my passion. When I explored mine, it was necessary to look at difficult situations and feelings, including my own bad behavior. Yet, doing this in my own life, looking at those feelings and that bad behavior, set me free.

One especially difficult portion of my journey was early sobriety. I discuss what I went through when I hit bottom. There are references throughout the book to my sober difficulties and successes. However, in no way is what I write intended to only address those of you who are drinking or in recovery. This book is *not* about alcoholism or recovery, even though reading some of my experiences could help you out if you're in recovery or desire to get into recovery.

I write for anyone who is angry or resentful; these are the keys, the qualifiers, and the issues that will be presented. It just so happens I drank and it deeply inflamed my anger. Once sober, I became a voracious reader about all things affecting me, including trauma, grief, and anger.

One thing I gained from my reading was the understanding of emotions *underneath* anger, and the knowledge to look beyond angry and resentful feelings for them. Once I identified these, my task became healing them. If you hold fast to anything you read in this book, please remember these two things I uncovered...

1. Forgiveness heals the hurt that forms the core of the wound under your anger.
2. When you forgive, anger toward a specific incident can be transcended, actually risen above.

Our society could use an understanding of how to reach forgiveness so as to reap the rewards of peace and freedom. We each benefit when we as individuals learn to manage our emotions, rather than acting them out or turning them inward. This knowledge is crucial to those who may, or have already, hurt someone. There needs to be a vehicle that people can utilize to get beyond the desire to harm, so the violence begins to end. Forever.

This book is such a vehicle. Those of us who have gotten beyond anger and resentment to all its rewards have a responsibility to share what we discovered with those who want to learn to get beyond *their* anger and resentment. In other words, those of us who have gotten beyond anger are called to pay forward our hard-earned wisdom. I am one such person who has resolved thirty years of anger, bitterness, and resentment. Even as I feel responsible to pay forward what I learned, it is with great passion that I do so. There is nothing more gratifying than hearing someone say they have been set free, based on a story or bit of knowledge I passed along. When I know he/she benefited from these things, it makes my heart soar to know another soul is flying free!

After careful consideration, I chose *The Art of Forgiveness: A Promise of Peace* as the title of the book. This was chosen in order to reflect the process, the evolution you go through to gain forgiveness. In other words, the title reflects the fact that learning to forgive is an art form. It's the creation of your masterpiece. Once you work through the art of forgiveness, there is a promise of peace.

For you who struggle with anger and resentment in your life as a result of your wounds, my intention is this book serves as a balm. What I share allows you to vicariously experience my journey as I venture through the art of forgiveness. It allows you to gain insight into my successes and failures. Again, if my experiences resonate with you, feel free to utilize in your own life what I've discovered in mine.

In closing, I wish you well as you meander through these pages. May they bring joy to your heart, a smile to your face, and especially peace and freedom to your soul!

Blessings, cj

Carolyn CJ Jones
San Francisco Bay Area
May 2019

PART I

Awakening

CHAPTER 1

Meltdown

"The deeper that sorrow carves into your being,
The more joy you can contain."
— Kahlil Gibran

The Beginning

It was a lovely day on the bay. As I sat in the sailboat tethered to the dock, the gentle waves lapped against the hull, soothing music to my ears. I looked forward to sharing some time with a dock mate I had grown to like. Imagine the shock when this person, the love of my life, the soul mate I'd searched for my entire *life*, blurted out angrily, "I have no feelings for you, no more than anyone else. I was just being kind."

I was blown away! I wanted to *vomit*. If I could have, I would have disappeared through the cockpit floor, to be swallowed up by the murky, frigid water below. I couldn't even defend myself from his false accusation that I'd told others we were in a relationship! This was the worst humiliation and shame I'd ever felt - *ever*. I suddenly realized I had put myself in the middle of a firestorm - one that *I created!* - by leaving my dysfunctional, alcoholic marriage for the man who had just spoken these debilitating and heart-crushing words.

That's *not* the way it was supposed to go! *My* plan was to sail into the sunset with this other guy and live happily together. After all, we worked well side-by-side on boat projects, and we could talk together at deep levels. There's more, of course, that led me to believe we were soul mates. Two hours earlier,

1

he was dancing around me with what appeared to be delight after a mutual dock mate friend told him I liked him. We belonged together, right?

Wrong. This rejection was the beginning of the end for me. Thirty years of drinking and drugging started unraveling. I was deeply devastated, paralyzed with pain. All I could do for two months was drink and cry over my humiliation, shame, and confusion; I couldn't even *feed* myself. I was so *sure* he cared! When he didn't, I lost touch with reality, didn't know what was real. I couldn't trust anything, especially my own thoughts and feelings.

You may be wondering at this point what an unrequited love has to do with forgiveness. Perhaps you're thinking, "Why are you telling me this?" Ah, the beautiful thing you'll discover about how to forgive is, it's a work of art. It evolves when you put in the time to create it, just as you would a piece of fine artwork - a brush stroke here… a stroke there… a change here… a tweak there… You are a work of art in progress, evolving over time. When you begin your healing journey, it's important to take the time to consider what wiped your canvas clean. This gives you a starting point, which is why I'm telling you my story. It defines the event that began my healing journey. As you read this chapter, you discover how I crawled out from under the pile of dirt that was suffocating me…

Surviving the Storm

This incident with the love of my life was quite a rude awakening. However, it was the part of my journey that *forced* me to begin my own artwork, my own healing. It led me to leave a difficult relationship and get sober. Over time, it has created a life that's resulted in my growth beyond the anger and resentment I'd held for years. This has produced the peace that I here-to-fore thought I'd found while drinking and doing drugs. I had no clue what peace was back then.

After the scolding in the cockpit, I hit bottom. Three months later, I desperately sought sobriety. This was the beginning of seven years sober during which time I felt the most excruciating emotional pain I had ever experienced. It was as if I was falling off a cliff into an abyss, with nothing to grab on to and no one to catch me. I was so terrified it took my breath away.

Never have I cried so many tears over the grief of a rejection. They were shed during my sober years, in addition to those spilled during those two months when I drank myself into oblivion. Once sober, I feared slipping into drinking again to obliterate these feelings. This fear led to a dogged perseverance to remain sober by going to meetings and doing the work I was asked to do. I also worked to heal the pain by pursuing and devouring books to bring me comfort, lift my spirit, and educate me. The pain ended because I went through the process of forgiveness, the same process through which I guide you in this book. In addition, pain further ended when I learned to be grateful for the debacle's role in my life.

Shoveling Off the Dirt

Although the unrequited love situation created the worst months and years of my lifetime, currently life has evolved into the deepest joy, peace, gratitude, and positivity I've ever known, let alone knew existed. Initially, I gained a feeling of peace and freedom when I discovered how to forgive my past at four years sober. It was at seven years of sobriety when my grief for the unrequited love was finally resolved. I discovered a book by Dr. Fred Luskin, Ph.D., titled *Forgive for Good*. It showed me how to be grateful for the heart-wrenching experience.

I also discovered the work of authors Ms. Mary Beth Sammons, and Ms. Nina Lesowitz. In their book, *Living Life As a Thank You,* they discuss how to transcend resentment using gratitude. They say, "Living each day as a thank you can help transform fear into courage, anger into forgiveness, isolation into belonging, and another's pain into healing. Saying thank you every day inspires feelings of love, compassion, and hope." The things referenced in this quote all have occurred for me. They can happen for you also. Gratitude, with forgiveness, is *that* powerful.

Over time and after I learned forgiveness and gratitude, deep feelings of joy, peace, and freedom came to me. This is the state in which I find myself today, pretty much continuously. It's truly a miracle, given my history of resentment, blaming, and negativity.

By learning gratitude for the unrequited love debacle, I learned to be grateful for everything in my life - *all* of it. As you learn to forgive yourself and others, plus to live in gratitude, you too, become blessed with the extraordinary feelings of peace and freedom. You may want to give up the journey along the way, especially when it comes to exploring your emotions, your feelings; I surely did. I invite you to resist any desire to quit your healing, perhaps your recovery, as the rewards are *exquisite.* Besides, you will never resolve those feelings if you don't look at them. They live on in the background, influencing and affecting everything you do in your life.

Ms. Robin Casarjian, M.A., states in her book, *Houses of Healing,* "...the old anger keeps playing itself out until the hurt and anger are dealt with." Again, what she describes is exactly what happened for me that led to the peace and freedom of which I speak. It all happened because I looked at, explored, and dealt with hidden feelings - feelings I had buried deep inside. Per Ms. Casarjian, "The secrets that you keep locked away keep you shame-ful…"

She also claims, "Keeping secrets deadens a part of us and stops the healing of our emotions and spirit." My spirit was clearly dead from all the things I had buried in my heart, in my soul. Was I scared to look at myself, my feelings? Terrified! Yet, there was no other choice to get beyond the resentment. Well, I had a choice. It was to get beyond the anger or not get beyond it. My current feelings would keep me an angry and bitter woman. I chose to free my spirit.

Another point about working through emotions and not quitting comes from Dr. Jim Dincalci. In his book, *How to Forgive When You Can't*, he notes, "Feelings might resurface as you start looking at your upsets and you might not want to continue. This is just a smoke screen put up by fear. In nature, the hunted will often turn to fight. When monstrous situations from the past haunt you mercilessly, attack is sometimes the best defense. If you are committed to slaying your demons and facing them head on, they will lose their power to frighten or harm you." This insight is useful for us all. May it urge you forward if fear appears.

It's interesting that God, a force and presence I had long ago abandoned because I believed He abandoned me in my early years, showed up now in my life. It was the book, *Conversations with God: An Uncommon Dialogue* by Neale Donald Walsch that began to wake me up. In it, he spoke, and speaks, of how God is in everything and everyone, in all situations and events, available through all mediums. Having read this book just before becoming sober, I came to sobriety alert and searching for God in people, in events - in literally everything. I began to hear messages in songs and to see them on billboards. I heard and saw things like, "Carry On!" and "You're on the right path." This is how God, that I currently call Spirit, worked and works for me; it can do the same for you. Furthermore, you can call that force anything that resonates with you, such as God, Allah, Higher Power, or Supreme Being.

Actually, it's become very apparent Spirit has been with me through *all* of my life's experiences - in my childhood difficulties, my dysfunctional marriage, the unrequited love situation, and the discoveries of treasures in sobriety. I just didn't know it, couldn't recognize it as a child. As an adult, I was in a haze from the substances I was abusing. Once sober, although I had some trust in Spirit, I trusted only so far and then took charge. Because of this, I was unable to totally live with Spirit until three or four years ago. Once I understood it had been divine guidance and intervention at work throughout my entire lifetime, and understood the reasons for the experiences, I gained trust. After this, Spirit became an integral part of my life.

With my drinking, I spiraled down after the sailboat encounter. The realization slowly dawned there was no going back and I was alone in the world; I became *terrified!* More beers... It also dawned on me I was killing myself from drinking, literally getting closer to death. The pain in my side had become constant and even *more* stabbing. I feared my liver was shot and I was slowly dying.

As I seriously considered this, I realized I didn't want to die, not *really*. The next thing I knew, I walked outside to the back of the boat where I was living at the time, raised my hands toward the heavens, and pleaded with God, if one existed, to please help. "I can't *do* this anymore!" was my anguished cry. Within three months, I was traveling to San Diego to stay for a couple of weeks and "get a handle on my drinking." I stayed for one-and-a-half years and got sober.

Receiving Gifts

Despite the ability to maintain sobriety, I continued grieving about the unrequited love. Finally at seven years, I learned about the wisdom and miracle of gratitude. It led me to my ability to get beyond the grief from the whole experience. This came about because of Dr. Luskin's book that taught me not only about gratitude, but how to manage a resentment as well. In *Forgive for Good,* he states how, when you have a resentment, you are doing three things. You are:

1. Taking the offense too personally,
2. Blaming the offender for how you feel, and
3. Telling a grievance story, a tale of woe.

Dr. Luskin discusses how to deal with the first two behaviors. I cover this in detail in Chapter 6, *Anger, Resentment, and Beyond.* It was the third point that resonated with me, and specifically, the recommended questions to ask myself in an effort to get beyond the grievance story I was telling. Dr. Luskin suggests answering three questions in order to get past the woeful tale. These questions are *extremely* powerful. When you utilize them, they work to gain gratitude and resolve resentment. Ask and answer:

1. What is the lesson I learned from the experience?
2. What is the positive that has occurred as a result of the offense?
3. What can I be grateful for?

After I realized these questions helped me feel better when I applied them to a resentment, I wondered if they would work on my grief from the rejection. I asked and answered the questions and they worked! I saw the whole unrequited love debacle with appreciation and gratitude. These questions worked *so well* for me, as they changed my perception of the event from negative and hurt to positive, uplifting, and almost celebratory. At a minimum, I understood the need for the experience.

Dr. Luskin's questions *totally* shifted my mindset. In fact, I discovered four things from the whole situation that were positives, as well as gratitudes. I realize as I write this book there is a fifth result from the whole unpleasant experience. These five miracles were, and continue to be, *amazing*, given my prior level of grief.

1. The debacle *pried* me out of my alcoholic marriage.
2. The whole situation prompted me to get sober after thirty years of hard drinking.
3. The unrequited love led me to forgive my past.
4. The rejection guided me to the forgiveness work I do today.
5. The experience allowed me to write this book as an offering to you who struggle.

I invite you to try Dr. Luskin's three questions the next time you're upset about a situation. Perhaps you will discover, as I did, that the queries about the lessons learned, the positives gained, and the gratitudes, are tremendously helpful in getting past difficult feelings.

These questions were instrumental in turning my life around permanently because they put the situation into a broader perspective. Most importantly, the questions allowed me to see the grief-producing experience with gratitude and positivity. Today, I recognize how *much* of a gift it was to discover the three questions. Doing so released me from the confusion and pain I had felt for those seven years following the unrequited love's rejection.

Prior to learning Dr. Luskin's questions to overcome a grievance, I often ranted to my spiritual advisor that sobriety wasn't worth it. I'd claim my drinking life was *much* better than my life was sober! I said this due to the fact that when I was drinking, I held down high-level, respected positions and got rave reviews as a registered nurse. At home, I was highly functional and productive in the evenings and on weekends with my husband, as we completed renovations on two each of homes, cars, and boats. Even though I got drunk at home every night during that time, I demonstrated I could function very well. In fact, I was able to produce excellent work. Sober, I couldn't even hold down a job! This was all very well and good, but my claim drinking was better than sobriety was a hasty judgment. It proved to be incorrect and *totally* false.

Drinking is *not* better than sobriety! Please also know that sobriety for me, when much of the healing work had been done, when gratitude had settled in, was and is, far, far, *far* better than my life drinking. There is not even a comparison! I never want to go back! This, coming from someone who during her drinking days, determined all her actions and plans based on whether or not alcohol would be served at an occasion. Then, she elected not to go places where there would be none. For thirty years she did this! Of course, I'm describing myself. It demonstrates how dependent I was on alcohol.

Managing Feelings

Pain prompts us to act to get away from it, to avoid it. For years, I pulled away from pain - numbed it - by using substances until they were no longer an option. Today, without my "friends" on which to rely, I handle my feelings much differently. Actually, because I now live in a space of gratitude and positivity, I don't often have difficult feelings. When I do, it has become possible for me to get beyond them by writing myself through them, and then talking to someone about what I wrote. Sometimes, I merely talk with Spirit -

out loud.

Shortly after I left San Diego, I returned to the Bay Area and proceeded to get a job at a boating store. It was there I injured my dominant hand, rendering it too painful to write. Yet, I *desperately* needed to journal and express my thoughts, so I wrote, actually printed, with my non-dominant hand. When I did this, profound thoughts spilled onto the page. In fact, three quarters of the inspirational verses that appear in my multi-award-winning, self-published book, *Opening the Gates of the Heart: A Journey of Healing,* came from my left-handed journals.

Jeff Rose claims in an article for *Good Financial Cents,* "There are studies that show that when you use your dominant hand, one hemisphere of the brain is active. When you use the non-dominant hand, both hemispheres are activated, which may result in thinking differently and becoming more creative." This was certainly the case for me with my "other" hand journaling.

After writing, I made it a point to talk with another about what I'd written. In current day, it is important to talk with someone else about my thoughts and feelings, someone in addition to Spirit. This is true for you as well. It is due to the fact that when you relay your thoughts and feelings to another person about what happened, it takes the power away from your destructive emotions. Also, as you talk it through with the other person, it may sound different to your ears when said out loud. You might pick up on something about the situation you didn't realize. Or, it might not sound as serious or as troubling as you originally thought. When you select someone in whom to confide, choose a person who will not ridicule, belittle, judge, or negate your feelings, beliefs, or experiences in any way. This is paramount!

Writing and then verbalizing difficulties allows you to choose how you wish to respond further to your feelings. Writing and talking with someone also encourages you to recognize and acknowledge the part of yourself who celebrates the kind and loving things you did and do for others and yourself. Learning what these things are can be achieved through a self-appraisal. It is an excellent exercise that yields very useful information about yourself. It allows you to identify not only the kind and loving things you've done, but the unloving, unkind, and maybe even mean behavior you've doled out to others *and/or* yourself. When needed, you apologize and provide compassion to the other and yourself for the pain you caused. Then you work on preventing its occurrence again.

You, like me, may have difficulty identifying your unkind and unloving traits, but what about positive ones? They're almost worse. Listing positive things about myself is something I was unable to do for several years in sobriety, as all I could see was the negativity I held. Additionally, I was unclear what I was feeling. Over time, however, and with much therapy, prayer, and perseverance, it became known to me that at my core, I am a kind and loving person. This is who I am. It is who we all are at our core. It is who *you* are at your very center. Unfortunately, I find that many people do not ever reach this point of self-realization and celebration. What I've witnessed is a minimizing of skills and abilities, especially by women. Having done this myself, I can truly say when you find forgiveness and gratitude at a deep level, you begin to see yourself with forgiving eyes and grateful heart. You see your strengths and gifts, *and* you begin to accept praise for them...

In stark contrast to the way in which I currently manage feelings are the years I drank and became a cynical, highly critical, and negative person. I was an angry, bitter, blaming victim, all over my childhood and my marriage. I blamed everyone and everything for my unhappiness. If you didn't act as desired, I got angry with you and became resentful. I had not yet learned it was my job to be responsible for my feelings, or that happiness came from within me. I didn't realize it was up to *me* to create it. Thankfully, I now know I have charge over my beliefs, reactions to feelings, and my own happiness. These are my responsibility, mine to manage.

Even though I may have been angry with someone, seething inside over a situation because it didn't work out the way I wanted it to, what I *actually* felt was hurt, disappointment, and fear, always fear. According to an article in *Healthpsych* magazine, anger is a secondary emotion that is fueled by feelings such as hurt, disappointment, humiliation, shame, sadness, fear, and loss or the anticipation of loss.

Today, knowing this information, I am remembering more and more to look for the feelings that led, or lead, to my anger. I acknowledge the sting of the feelings, without judgment, and then become still while they pass through me. I get to the point when I can explore them with curiosity. "Isn't that interesting?" I say to myself. "I wonder why I did this? What was behind it?" You can begin to explore your resentment with great curiosity. When you think about considering your actions and behaviors as an investigator might, it takes away the shame. After you've identified your feelings, you can work through the emotion instead of acting it out through bad behavior. This also prevents you from turning it inward in despair, while engaging in destructive self-talk and self-treatment. The key is the willingness to go within. It's very empowering to do so, and adds to the level of your personal, inner peace.

Ms. Casarjian tells us in *Houses of Healing*, until we look within, there is an unconscious compulsion on our part to keep repeating the same behaviors that made our lives unmanageable in the past. She claims, "Until the inner child's pain is honored - like it or not - we keep replaying the same old story." Furthermore, she believes acknowledging the neglect, disrespect, and abuse from the point of view of both your adult Self and your inner child leads to emotional healing. She recommends you go back to your childhood to finish the work that wasn't completed as a child or up to this point as an adult.

It is important to do this work, Ms. Casarjian notes. If you don't deal with negative emotions, you continue with negative self-talk, self-hatred, shame, feelings of emptiness, and possibly even depression. By looking back and doing the work, you can move forward to self-respect, freedom, and creative power. When I say, "...doing the work," I mean working through feelings like we are doing in this book – working through the art of forgiveness.

This is not to say that when you look back, when you look within, you become mired in the old feelings. On the contrary; choose to visit the past only to identify, acknowledge, and feel your feelings from the hurts and slights you suffered. Do not remain there. Look to identify the feelings for which your inner child needs comfort. After you feel those feelings and offer comfort, return to the present. Look at the experience with introspective curiosity, for when you do so, it helps you avoid wallowing in anger, resentment, grief, or sorrow.

Ms. Casarjian writes when you don't do the inner work of re-parenting and healing yourself, you attract a mate who will - you think - heal your wounds. This never works. My marriage is a shining example. In Chapter 2, you'll see why I say this. To re-parent yourself, she recommends first getting in touch with your healthy inner adult - your Self. Allow this part of you to feel and then acknowledge the pain. Ask your inner child to join you in sharing his/her hurts, fears, and pain. Comfort him/her. Get in touch with your adult Self by journaling every day. Write to your child, and share respect, comfort, and safety. To hasten the process of healing your inner child, you can write your Self's words with your dominant hand and print your inner child's words with your non-dominant hand.

Choosing Rewards

The thing about forgiveness is you can get to a point where you *yearn* for peace and freedom from your resentment. You can choose to experience these feelings and not your resentment. This started occurring for me at some point I don't recall. I had become tired of being angry all the time. The bitter taste in my mouth had soured. I desired these rewards *so much*, that I graciously did what I needed to do. I had chosen the path of forgiveness and gratitude for everything, and peace and freedom found me. You, too, can choose to take the journey to forgiveness because you want peace and freedom more than you want the anger and bitterness or the stress and chaos. If this is what you desire, I am hopeful this book supports you to get to the point of finding that place you seek.

Aside from my sobriety, there are two reasons I'm able to write this book in current day. One is due to the discovery of forgiveness for my past. The other is a direct result of learning how to be grateful for *all* of my lifetime experiences. This occurred roughly three or four years ago and was a tremendous revelation. Then, years after I became able to forgive others, I began to work on forgiving myself. I find even today, I have to frequently forgive what I've done or said. I discovered forgiving myself throughout the day keeps me peaceful and prevents the development of a resentment, one that is often against myself.

Some people have to forgive themselves before they can forgive another. This was not my experience; I forgave my offender before I forgave myself. Therefore, I cannot speak to the issues you may encounter if you have the need to forgive yourself first. Ultimately, the key is to discover self-forgiveness in addition to forgiveness of another, regardless of which precedes the other.

As we close this chapter, think about any soul-shattering moment that rocked your world. Have you healed from it? I invite you to write about how you coped with such an experience. In other words, get curious about how you managed an emotional meltdown. Did you hide from it, explore it, or write about it? Define what was useful for you. I invite you to use your "other" hand when writing so you can bring up some really revealing things. Write about it now if you haven't healed. Happy "other" hand writing!

CHAPTER 2

Ending a Marriage

"An unrealistic expectation is a
Resentment waiting to happen."
— Richard Rohr

Setting the Stage

Now that you're familiar with my crashing meltdown, you
may be wondering why I felt so compelled to leave my
marriage. After all, it had been twenty years, so what
prompted me to leave at that point? That's the subject of this
chapter. From it, you gain an understanding of what married
life was like for me.

To be honest, there were many, many times our marriage
was delightful and fun. Much of that was when we were
drinking and drugging. The "fun," however, turned into
verbal and emotional attacks against each other the drunker
we became. When the fellow dock mate showed up in my life
and I developed feelings for him, I cast aside my marriage
and left to make myself available to this new, wonderful man.

I didn't do this lightly, mind you. In fact, I *agonized* over my
feelings for the dock mate exactly because I *was* married. I
didn't want to hurt my husband! I spent two hours every day
for many months, journaling about my thoughts and what to
do, wondering if the dock mate was showing signs of liking
me, too, wondering how to manage my marriage. Eventually,
I concluded the other man was acting like a man who liked
me and the marriage was irretrievable. I found a little house
to rent and committed to move off our boat.

It's sad I never spoke with the dock mate about my feelings. It might have saved years of grief for all involved. I was unable to do that in those days. It took many years of therapy and recovery before I could even *recognize* what I was feeling, let alone express it to another. Interestingly, I *did* journal about my feelings, or so I thought. Instead, it was a lot of questioning and replaying of hurts, disappointments, and confusion. There was a teaching moment in the whole debacle. Knowing to speak with someone if I were to develop romantic feelings for them is one of those "lessons learned" from the three questions to which Dr. Luskin refers, as discussed in Chapter 1.

My sadness extends to my inability to speak to my husband throughout our marriage about my feelings toward him. I loved him the only way I knew to love. Even so, at the end, I felt beaten down and unable to cope in the relationship any longer. Come back in time as I explain...

After growing up and graduating from college in Ohio, I moved to Colorado. This is where my future husband and I hooked up. We got together while we were both living in a ski town in the Colorado Rockies. In addition to looks and personality, I was attracted because he did the same things I did - he drank and did drugs. We met at a Willie Nelson concert in a bar. Once we started hanging out, there was no one on my back telling me to quit or get control. We partied together and had some great times I'll always treasure. Yet, we were out of control.

Our drinking and drugging was heavy and dysfunctional from the beginning. It led to frequent arguments fraught with verbal and emotional onslaughts. I had threatened to leave for years, yet, never did. I was too fearful of being alone. Years later, I am aware of how destructive this was of me to stay in the relationship when I knew it wasn't feeding my heart and soul. Doing so led to the denigration of my soul and that of my husband. I am sad about this, yet, am grateful to have become aware so I won't repeat it with someone else.

There are examples of how my ex-husband's behavior toward me slowly ground away at my self-esteem and worth. Here is some background...

I have been blessed with the ability to do finish work on various pieces of wood. I watched my mother refinish all sorts of pieces; she excelled at refinishing furniture. My sister retired from a career of rebuilding and refinishing pianos, so maybe the skill is in our blood. In my own right, in the future I would become known at a marina for my varnishing of teak trim on boats. The refinished wood reflected like a mirror and the depth of the grain was endless...

There came a point in 1982 when my husband and I grew tired of the cold and snow, and left the mountains in favor of the Denver area. Over the years, we got involved with renovating the kitchens and baths in our two homes. We each had our areas of expertise. Mine was the wood refinishing and painting. Sometimes, when I'd done a project, my husband praised me to friends. Later, he became angry I had taken the time to do it. He was upset I was working a part time job while also keeping up on the reconstruction projects. He wanted me working full time. His anger was confusing and crazy making because we had agreed before I went part time, I would do so in order to have time to work on renovation projects in addition to working at my nursing. (I worked as a nurse case manager out of our family room.) This issue was never resolved.

In 1997, we moved from Colorado to the San Francisco Bay Area to live aboard a forty-five-foot traditional sailboat. We negotiated again. We agreed I would work part time for my nursing - with the same company - and do the boat reconstruction projects part time. He didn't recall this conversation; it was a source of frequent fights.

Repeatedly, I watched him step *on* the teak trim I had varnished as he stepped on the boat, instead of stepping *over* it to preserve it and prevent scratches. It was highly deflating to watch this happen again and again, despite my requests he step over the varnished piece. It felt like a lack of respect for my work and for me. I stopped bringing it up, as an argument usually ensued.

Over time, I downplayed my skills when my husband praised my work to our friends. If another complimented me for something I'd worked on, I pointed out the flaws. Doing that for myself took its toll. Have you ever downplayed your abilities, played dumb to prevent negative consequences from occurring when you show pride in your accomplishments? How'd it work out for you? Take some time and write about feeling less than you are, if it applies. For example, what was that like for you to minimize your abilities?

After you write about downplaying your talents, write one thing for which you praise yourself in current day. Write your accomplishments with that one situation. I invite you to remember *this* and apply it to all the things in which you engage. In other words, recognize and own your skills. Be grateful for them. There is no further need to minimize yourself and your talents.

I worked for twenty-seven years in the nursing profession. Once, while employed as a nurse resource consultant by a state's Medicaid department, I took the lead in creating a new, special program that allowed medically fragile, technology-dependent children to live at home with the assistance of private duty nursing care instead of living in the hospital's intensive care unit. It changed the course of these children's lives. My husband had grown tired of hearing frequently told details of the program and its development; I took this too personally and was hurt by it. In sharing my enthusiasm about my groundbreaking work at the State, a visiting relative responded, "A *real* nurse would work in the ER or ICU!"

These words and my husband's lack of interest deflated my confidence and gnawed away at my self-esteem. It affected the feeling that I was being of use to these children. I was ashamed I was not a "real" nurse. I was *so* ashamed that for many, many years, I could not claim my role, my part, in the creation of a safe place at home for these fragile children in the special program. In fact, I thought my whole involvement in the design, development, and management of the program was minimal and unimportant. I gave credit to the Advisory Board I'd created, as well as the providers of care. Even though the advice I received from both enriched the program, I totally negated what I had accomplished in my role.

Growth

Currently, my worth is no longer attached to being a "real" nurse, or to being a nurse at all. It feels wonderful to have changed the lives of many children. They are adults now and I frequently wonder how they are and what they're doing. Nor is my worth dependent upon another's thoughts about what I'm doing or have done - most days anyway. Rather, it's attached to things such as acknowledging the blessings and positives brought to me by Spirit in any given moment. These are mixed with thoughts about what's on my calendar for the day, what's happening in my business, what's right in front of me to do, who I need to talk with...

In other words, I try my best to live in the present moment, while going into the future enough to plan things and set goals. I feel more connected to others when I'm in the present, in the here and now. On the other hand, I do, like all of us, have my dreams. In my mind and heart, I visualize mine. For example, some day I'd like to spend time in the Caribbean on a sailboat, varnishing teak. I picture myself there, smelling the familiar, pungent scent of varnish and feeling the sandpaper roughing up my fingertips. After I "experience" this, I forget about it, sometimes for weeks or months - even years. I have every reason to believe this will one day become reality. Dreams have come to life for me several times over the years, usually after I have forgotten about my desire. Then, in the course of the choices I've made, I realize a dream has been fulfilled.

Certainly, I think back on the past about the years of my marriage. I think about my behavior during various angry situations in which I resented my husband. As I go back in time, I look without blame, with an attitude of curiosity instead of shame, guilt, or judgment. Mind you, that attitude took me a while to adopt – years. What I've discovered when I looked is, I did my share of starting arguments.

I first realized nearly three years ago my behavior was a part of our falling apart. Every once in a while, thoughts of my ex-husband cross my mind. One day, I felt guilty for the poor way I handled the marriage. After all, I blamed him when it was also me. This evolved into embarrassment, followed by a thirst to know more. It seemed the more I looked, the less attached to it I felt; I could be objective about my behavior. The end result was great empowerment. I knew and understood the feelings underneath my bad behavior. I had the knowledge I could change that behavior. For this, I was grateful. By focusing on gratitude, I resolved remorse for the way I treated my husband. I forgave myself. *This* was empowering. You can create this type of attitude in your life, too, through the practices of gratitude and forgiveness.

My husband and I were not equipped to be in a relationship, let alone be married. I know I wasn't. For us, alcohol simply inflamed and intensified the hurt of wounds we each brought to the union. The problem was, the feelings under the wounds were disguised as anger and resentment. Here again, thank you, Spirit, for my feelings toward the unrequited love. It's the *only* thing that got me to leave a difficult situation. I got away from the liquor and the put-downs to grow and heal. Sometimes, I get sad for the way I left, as it was extremely hurtful. I don't know if my ex-husband has healed enough to let it go in favor of peace and freedom. I am hopeful he has.

The Toll of Rejection

Ages twenty-two to forty-eight were spent drinking and drugging. My drink was Miller Lite cans with the occasional side cocktail – margarita, bloody mary, or mimosa. I have been known to resort to drinking scotch, my ex-husband's drink, and cooking sherry. My drug of choice for a decade was cocaine. One day in the mid-90s, I decided I didn't want to do it anymore. I was tired of the effect; eventually, I stopped buying it.

The alcohol turned on me years before the unrequited love debacle occurred. In fact, it turned on me from the very beginning when I had my first drinking experience during senior year in college. My roommates tried to console me by getting me drunk after I learned my fiancée had married someone else. Hmmm. Rejection seems to be a theme in my life. It certainly took its toll…

According to Ms. Maura McCarley Torkildson, M.A., in her blog, *Tackling Trauma*, "…rejection is one of the most hurtful experiences a human can face, belonging is so important to our well-being." Having been rejected by a fiancée and the unrequited love, I had faced a great deal of hurt that resulted in a deep and wide wound.

As I read Ms. Torkildson's words, I fully understood why my feelings for the love debacle were so difficult and had lasted so long. In addition to the rejection from my "soul mate," the debacle served as a trigger for my previous wound. There were countless years of shame, worthlessness, lack of confidence, and more negative things about myself that needed to be overcome. It was all coming to the surface so I could heal at the very core of the wound.

I believe there are wounds underlying one's anger and resentment. Once you look at and sooth your wound, you can learn to accept it as you consider the beauty in everyone's diversity and uniqueness. You can offer compassion and empathy to one who has been rejected, as you now understand what that feels like. Offering compassion and empathy applies to the offender too, as they also experience the effects of rejection.

It's important that healing of wounds begins to happen as part of the art of forgiveness. I found it impossible, for example, to just forgive when I hadn't started to heal. Some healing needed to occur before forgiveness could happen. The unhealed emotions got in the way of me attaining forgiveness. Without doing a little healing work, I really wasn't able to forgive. Just by saying I forgave someone was a bit like when I drank. I was sweeping aside and pretending feelings, only this time, it would be pretending forgiveness. The positive in this is, once you begin to understand your wounds and the feelings beneath them, ultimate healing happens when you find it in your heart and soul to forgive.

To heal, I invite you to start by identifying your feelings. Name them. While I was seeking help around six years sober, I did not know what I was feeling. My therapist printed out a list of emotions from which I could choose a feeling at any given moment. Brilliant! And it worked! I began to identify and name my feelings. You see, throughout my life, I pushed my emotions down deep inside and was no longer able to know them. Maybe you've done this, too, and have difficulty retrieving your feelings. I invite you to try finding a list of emotions to use as a reference. It can open your world.

Once I had a name for what I was feeling, I started seeing myself described in the literature. I began to discover how each feeling might have originated, and how to heal it. In retrospect, this time period was a turning point. I learned to view my feelings and situations with some objectivity. When you can feel your feelings without judgment, embarrassment, or shame, they pass through you. As a result, you can deal with them more easily.

After my college fiancée wrote to me of his marriage, that first drink began my spin out of control. I drank to excess to numb a very bruised self-esteem and a great lack of confidence. This, in turn, elevated the feelings of anger, shame, and worthlessness I'd developed over my early years.

When I drank, I felt valuable and valued. Alcohol gave me the bravery I lacked, the esteem and confidence I craved. It gave me courage to be a nurse. I felt uncomfortable being responsible for others' lives. When faced with continuing in the profession or staying sober, I chose sobriety. I didn't think I could be a nurse and not drink. I also chose sobriety so I would never go back to the misery I felt over the unrequited love.

I Don't Have No Stinkin' Drinkin' Problem!

We've established alcohol usage was a problem in my marriage. After six years in the Denver area, our friends pleaded with us to stop drinking and drugging. One evening, a friend took my husband and me to a twelve-step meeting. We judged and criticized the attendees harshly, even laughed at them after the meeting for being so weak-willed - they couldn't just stop. They needed to keep coming and coming to meetings. We also smirked at them for drinking so much coffee. Today I must be a great alcoholic because I *love* my coffee. We then proceeded to ignore our friends' pleas and continued with our lives, drinking and drugging every evening after work. I am happy we never drank on the job or went in drunk.

As I look back, my disdain for the people at the meeting brings a deep sadness. I had no understanding about the disease of alcoholism, didn't know not drinking wasn't a matter of willpower, for example. It had nothing to *do* with willpower. Yet, knowing nothing about their situation, I judged so harshly. I knew not a thing about these people and, yet, I acted superior to them. Let me repeat this for emphasis. I knew nothing about these people and still, I judged and acted superior to them.

There is a lesson to be learned here for all of us. I invite you to determine if judgments and feelings or actions of superiority are occurring for you. I further invite you to list one person you currently judge; write down your judgment(s) of them, as well as why you're superior. Now set these aside for a minute. Next, consider your beliefs about this human being. Ask yourself, who are they as a person? Are they kind, loving, tolerant, respectful of themselves and others? Do we even *think* of these types of things when we look at someone? I don't think we do at all. Instead, I think our minds are busy judging them first by color, then clothes, then tattoos and hair – their physical appearance. Eventually, the maligning of their culture and religion begins. I observe this time and again.

Could we, could you and I, stop when we start to judge another? Could I, could you, take the time to be curious who this person is as a being? A mother, daughter, husband, son? Are they kind and loving people? As diversity continues to grow in the nation and the world, we as societies can choose to consider another in this manner, or hold hate for and remain resentful of anyone different than us. That'll continue to make for an angry planet.

It seems like today, many take little or no time to learn of another's beliefs, customs, or thoughts. We simply judge them as not worthy of our respect, our kindness, our caring. The truth about me acting superior to the folks at the meeting was, I felt very *inferior* to them. Frequently, when we feel "less than," inferior, or lacking, we become self-righteous and "better than" another. That's what I did in this example. The other thing is, in my recovery, I have been to literally thousands of meetings and have learned the attendees are fine, kind-hearted and loving people. They return to meetings over and over because they're highly inspiring to attend.

One more thing… I was one of "them." I just wouldn't allow myself to go there on a conscious level. What really happened was I avoided looking at alcoholics and their plight because that would mean I'd have to look at myself. I couldn't see the bumper sticker "Live and Let Live" without becoming uncomfortable, as I knew it was a slogan for alcoholics. Deep down, I knew I had a problem, yet, was terrified to live without liquor. I couldn't imagine how I'd ever be able to do that, so I didn't look, just continued to avoid. When *Hillstreet Blues*, my favorite TV series in the 80s that I never missed, had Captain Furillo's character become a recovering alcoholic, I never watched again. I could not tolerate the reflection in the mirror.

Neither my husband nor I felt we had drinking problems. "How could I, if I were an alcoholic, be holding down this highly respected position?" we'd each state indignantly. We were well praised for our performances at our respective jobs. In my years as a registered nurse, I worked mostly in administrative positions. This included the time when I worked at the State and developed that special program for the children. It was because of my ability to design and run the Private Duty Nursing program, and the rave performance evaluations I received at my jobs, that led me to deny I had a drinking problem. Furthermore, as I mentioned, my husband and I were productive renovating the houses, working on our twenty-six, and then forty-five, foot sailboats, and restoring older cars. It took the unrequited love situation and drinking myself into oblivion for two months to get my attention and jar me into becoming sober. This ultimately led to forgiveness and gratitude.

Developing gratitude for a difficult experience helps to transcend that situation. I don't say this lightly. For example, it took me seven years of sobriety and great anguish before I read Dr. Luskin's *Forgive for Good*. I discovered his work turned my tale of woe into a hero's song. From it, I realized I could think about the unrequited love from a different perspective. I could *choose* to look at the situation differently. It was up to me. I chose to see gratitude. Years later, I saw the miracle, the divine intervention, at work when I discovered this. You, too, have the power to choose your attitude. I invite you to choose what brings you peace and freedom, what makes your heart sing.

Choosing to Look Within

Perhaps the most beneficial and empowering thing I've gained over the years is learning how to look within and perform a self-appraisal. This involves looking with curiosity and acceptance of your behavior, without judgment. When you do an appraisal, be aware of slipping into shaming and judging yourself. These are non-productive. If you feel ashamed of your behavior, remember to identify the lesson you learned from your actions or words, the positive that's happening because of what you said or did, and the gratitude from the experience.

According to the National Institute for the Clinical Application of Behavioral Medicine, shame originates early in life. It leads to the feeling that you are not worthy as a person or that you have no right to take up people's time or space, for example. This is a feeling that, if left unattended, will likely develop into depression and/or substance abuse. To cope with any shame, give yourself compassion for the wounded child you were and are. Move your awareness away from self-criticism to self-praise. Make the choice to look within and miraculous things can begin to happen for you.

After any mindset shift that is needed - for example, achieving willingness - you are ready to do the appraisal of your behavior. I mention it here; further discussion is in the next chapter. To start, list four kind and loving things you did - two for another and two for yourself - in the last three days. Then list four unkind, unloving, and mean behaviors - two to others and two to yourself - in that same timeframe. When you do this exercise often, you notice a freedom and empowerment. You've seen yourself at your best and your worst. You *choose* to celebrate yourself. At the same time, you take what no longer works for you and *choose* to work on changing that behavior. This is highly empowering.

For me, the journey has been long and, at times, difficult. There were, however, positives the entire way. Today I see the benefit of all the struggles. The difficulties gave me a far better understanding of what others might be feeling because of my first-hand experience with similar situations. This has grown into my ability to be compassionate and empathetic, and to love and show kindness to others. I've even learned to show myself the same things. As you incorporate into your life the points you gain from this book, it is my desire you, too, learn compassion and empathy, as well as love and kindness for yourself and others.

When I started this journey, there was not even a spec on my radar that the type of peace, happiness, and freedom I now experience, existed. Yet, here I am, living in total peace and joy, happy and free from resentment. I am grateful beyond words! The journey is turning out beautifully, even though there were many difficult times.

I invite you to explore in writing any current situation that is troubling you. List your choices. Clarify your feelings about each choice. Perhaps you'll identify fear. If so, write about what's underneath it. If it's warning of danger, then heed it. If that's not the case, then looking it straight in the eye takes away the power fear has over you. After writing, speak with someone about how you feel regarding what you wrote. Be sure they can be trusted with your confidence. You might speak with a trusted friend or partner, a spiritual advisor or sponsor if you're in a twelve-step program, or clergy.

PART II

Rebirth

CHAPTER 3

Picking Up the Pieces

"Everyone has the same chance for happiness.
The only thing is whether we pay attention
And have sufficient awareness."
— The Dalai Lama

Asking for Help

As I have been sharing my story with you, I've been somewhat reliving the experiences about which I write. From that, a question has arisen. Why did I never reach out to anyone about my breakdown? Why did I never talk to anyone about my inability to care for myself? I decided to explore that issue in this chapter. I also discuss the experience that saved me. Finally, I speak of my early sobriety.

If you are like me, you learned asking for help was a sign of great weakness. I wonder if shame played a role in that not-asking-for-help arena? It's as if someone was saying, because you don't understand something, have a question, or need a hand, you're defective for some reason. At all costs, asking for help was to be avoided.

In *Houses of Healing*, Ms. Casarjian discusses shame and the role it plays in our inability to forgive. She relays that toxic shame, a shame that goes extremely deep, originates when our needs for basic love, security, safety, and caring attention are not met during the early months of life. It's not a feeling that we *did* something wrong. It's that *we* are wrong - defective as human beings. We cannot forgive ourselves when we feel this, as we do not deserve to be forgiven, or so we think. There is good news. These feelings of shame can be worked through, according to the National Institute for the Clinical Application of Behavioral Medicine. They recommend you engage in positive self-talk, affirming your worthiness as a person. NICABM has published recommendations on other healing methods that can be found on their website at www.nicabm.org.

It could be my reluctance to ask for help was due to an inability to receive from others. It is grace that allows you to receive from someone else - grace and humility. It is also feeling worthy enough to receive, worthwhile enough for assistance from another. On the flip side of feeling worthy is feeling unworthy. I spent a lifetime feeling worthless, explaining to people who had praised me why their perception and praise were misplaced, not true about me. It took a lot of awareness and paying attention to get to a point of feeling more deserving of accolades. I have finally learned to say, "Thank you," and mean it. No explanation of why I believe I am unworthy of the praise is needed from me, as I feel worthy. I am able to just take it in. Amazingly, doing this has led to an increased self-esteem and self-confidence.

Part of what stopped me from asking for help was my pride, my ego. I'd say to myself, "I *should* be able to handle this!" I invite you to be aware of the word "should." When you or someone else "shoulds" you, shame is often the response. It may even be an intentional shaming. As an example of being "shoulded," I have been repeatedly shamed in my life. I frequently encountered the comment, "You *should* know! You're a nurse!" I don't know if the shaming was intentional or if it was unconscious on the part of all the people who said this, yet, the effect was the same - instant shame. Guilt for not living up to what I was supposed to know followed closely on its heels. From that came more shame. I drank more...

Phrases to use other than ones including "should" might be, "I might have…" "You could have…" "Shall I…?" "I wish I would have…" The latter is a big one. We frequently have regrets over the way we did or said something. We wish we'd have done things differently. Have you ever experienced this? I would think you have, so you know the feeling of regret. Rather than hold that feeling, see it as a positive thing. Use it to grow. After all, you learned this is something you do not wish to repeat.

Can you feel the difference between "I *should* have," and "I wish I would have?" The former is almost as if you're shaking your finger at yourself. It allows you to beat up on yourself, whereas "I wish I would have…" allows you to state a desire, albeit with some probable disappointment, sadness, and/or regret. These can be resolved. The key is to choose gratitude for the lesson learned and for the positives that came because of the situation. Follow that up with determining how you would now do what you did differently, rather than getting swallowed by regret. Look forward with hope and excitement, for again, you've learned wonderful lessons you probably won't repeat. Accept the past. Grieve if needed, then let it be. Practice gratitude.

As far as being shamed by another, when someone is continually saying, "You *should* do this," and "You *should* do that," it's usually shaming. Positive self-talk helps to mitigate the occurrence of shame in response to the "shoulding" comments.

The Miracle of Brad

It was in a shame-based state after the meltdown on the sailboat that I found myself one day. Deep down, perhaps I felt I was not worth helping. Maybe that's why I didn't ask anyone to assist me, to help drag me up from the abyss in which I was living. I didn't dare tell anyone I was so depressed! What if they took me somewhere for a psych evaluation? I didn't want to be taken in.

One day, after two months of trying to manage my emotional status alone, the afternoon rolled around. I was at my usual three-o'clock spot – the deck bathed in sunlight at the local bar on the waterfront. I ordered my standard - two margaritas on the rocks, no salt. On this day, I settled in and began my customary afternoon and evening drunk. After I finished the drinks, I would be walking to the grocery store across the street for a six-pack of beer. Then I'd return to my dinghy and row back to the anchored sailboat where I lived. Later that night, I'd most likely row to shore to get a second six-pack. My mission was to obliterate my feelings. At the time, I had no clue this is what I was doing. All I knew was beer helped me cope by numbing my pain, so I drank.

Catching movement from the corner of my eye, I was roused from my thoughts. My attention switched back to the present moment. The guy on a bicycle with his dog running behind him approached. As was my habit every afternoon when he came by, I waved. This time was different, though, because instead of waving back, he stopped. He said hello, then asked if I was okay. "Sure. I'm fine," I responded with a smile and as much assuredness as I could muster. He looked at me and replied, "No. You're not." The torrent of tears was unstoppable; he waited patiently while I regained my composure. Then we talked.

Thus, began my road back to living, back to sanity. The time Brad took to be with me was a miracle. He gave me space to puzzle over my plight. He encouraged me to express my grief, regret over how I left my husband, fear of being alone in the world, and confusion about how I misread the other man's behaviors so completely. He offered safety, comfort, and a sense of reality. He truly did a very human thing, very compassionate, very caring. I am deeply grateful for Brad in my life and touch bases now and again even today.

Eventually, Brad redirected my attention to my passion of varnishing teak wood on boats. This was important to me, as at the time I found out the dock mate didn't care for me, I had a part time job varnishing the interior teak on a sailboat that was anchored at the marina. I had been unable to work on her for a few weeks due to my depression and being either drunk or hung over. Brad's gentle urging changed that. Actually, he asked me to teach him how to varnish and that's how he got me to return to it. Varnishing was meditative for me. I got totally engrossed in it and the rest of the world disappeared. It fed my soul and certainly healed my spirit. It was timely medicine.

A month had passed with Brad as a friend when the thought came to me to go on a road trip to "find myself." I learned this was an example of a Spirit-inspired thought. Having had this quiet thought that kept repeating itself, I listened. Years later, I interpreted it to be the voice of Spirit. It had been trying to get me to choose the journey intended for me. I chose well.

I started my plans for a trip to the southwest and Baja, Mexico - all in my little 1984 Audi 4000CS Quattro sedan... with 400,000 miles and going strong... hugged the road like an Indy car. Anyway, I planned to go to San Diego for a couple of weeks to stay with my old bartender. She lived there and was getting sober herself. I'd get that handle on my drinking and continue my trip. I had it all figured out.

The road trip became my focus. Suddenly, my life had a direction in which to move. I was excited and more positive. I began to recall my last road trip in the mid-70s when I drove round trip from Denver to Philadelphia. I learned how to be a courteous driver from the truckers. That trip is one reason I enjoy driving so much today. To prepare for living and tent camping out of the Audi, I took the back seat out to create storage space. Next, I put in plastic drawers for my clothes, pots, pans, and dishes. I bought a roof container for storing camping gear, such as a tent and so forth.

My soon-to-be ex-husband even pitched in and checked over the car. He was a German car mechanic and donated time to the cause. I was relieved and appreciated his assistance. Packed and ready to go, I drove away from the Bay Area, away from Marin County. I was *never* coming back! It held too many bad memories and the people were just too "out there." Interestingly, I now live in Marin where I own property and have good friends who are not odd or way out there.

A Second Chance

I enjoyed my meander down the coast. I took the time to stop and view the ocean, camp out, and roller blade. I drank myself to sleep every night with my routine six-pack. On March 5, 2001, I arrived in San Diego and searched for Ocean Beach where my friend lived. Before I knew it, I was in Chula Vista, on the southeast portion of San Diego. I needed to be on the northwest side of town. Exhausted, I rented a hotel room and had one more drunken cry about the unrequited love situation. I drank the last beer of the six-pack and passed out on the bed.

On March 6, 2001, I awoke, resolved that I would no longer drink. Thus, began the initially painful journey to live my life as a sober person. I did find my friend's place in Ocean Beach. We kept ourselves occupied and sober. After a week, she said to me, "I don't know about you, but I'm going to a twelve-step meeting. I've been to one before in another situation and it was very helpful. You're welcome to come with me or not."

I took this invitation as a sign from God to go to the meeting with her.

I'll never forget the small, brick church we went to for our first encounter. It was a candlelight gathering. I felt nervous to proclaim my drinking problem, yet, the words rolled effortlessly off my tongue. The backpack of rocks I carried emptied itself in that moment. An exquisite release!

We were fortunate there were four or five meetings a day within three blocks of our house. I ended up walking to three or four of them every day for a year-and-a-half. It's what I needed to do to keep myself sober in the midst of wrenching anguish over the unrequited love, regret over my marriage, and anger over childhood. All the feelings I'd kept at bay during my drinking years came rushing out of me. I had nothing to numb them. So much for staying a couple of weeks...

The other option, which would have most likely supported me through my healing more quickly, was an in-patient rehab. This was not something I felt I could do financially. Additionally, I'm a private mourner. Furthermore, it is unknown if I could have handled one emotion on top of another that might have occurred in a twenty-eight day rehab. I could have been overwhelmed and, in response, have shut down. At any rate, it happened just as it needed to happen.

More than eighteen years have passed since I lived aboard the sailboat and uttered those words to a God in whom I had no trust or belief. It is with awe that I realize how much that presence – God, Spirit, Higher Power – has helped me heal. As a result, I now live in deep peace with wonderful freedom and gratitude for everything. This gives me pause, as I recognize how very far I've come in my life. I'd like to share with you what I did to reach this attitude. To get to this point, I started with willingness to do three things. I became willing to:

1. Open up to the possibility that God/Spirit was guiding me and allow it to do so,
2. Become sober, and finally,
3. See and interpret things differently.

Over the years, I have believed Brad's notice of and attention to my breakdown was a miracle. His kind act of stopping to see how I was allowed my amazing recovery to begin. I now recognize his appearance in my life as an answer to my desperate prayer that night on the sailboat. Brad was sent by Spirit to save me from impending death. On my journey, I've been blessed with the ability to recognize this and share my life with Spirit, blessed to see miracles in my life. I am deeply grateful.

My passion in current day is sharing my story with you. From it, you can begin to see miracles through Spirit working in *your* life, answering *your* prayers. I feel called to connect with *each* of you through my words, through these pages. I invite you to be on the lookout for the ways in which Spirit graces your life.

Early Recovery

During the first six months or so I was sober, I was in such great emotional pain with my grief, regret, and anger, it led to a great deal of agitated energy. One defense was to desperately cling to the meetings I attended throughout the day. Another was to continue my morning walking routine and then write my heart out for two or three hours. I say, "continue," because my walking and journal writing were established a year earlier when I was still living on the boat with my husband. It developed when I started having feelings for the dock mate. My first journaling began when I got up at five o'clock a.m., tiptoed off the boat, and practically *ran* to the local bait shop on the waterfront. I got my steaming hot coffee and for two hours, sat outside and wrote down all my thoughts, concerns, and confusion. Then I tiptoed back onto the boat before my husband woke up.

In Ocean Beach, I continued the routine I established when I was married. Instead of walking to the bait shop, I walked to the ocean. There I sat on top of a seawall while I wrote about my thoughts. Words poured onto the pages about the confusion and hurt over the debacle, as well as anger and hurt over childhood experiences. After I finished, I returned to the house to read my eleven daily meditation books. I read so many in order to calm myself and soothe my feelings by instilling positive messages. In current day, eleven books would *overwhelm* me. I could only tolerate one, maybe two, yet these books would evoke a deep thought process.

Bedtime was the worst. Free to wander, my mind usually ended up going to the unrequited love, to my grief and confusion. I cried myself to sleep every night to the sounds of banjo and guitar playing classical-like music. Jens Kruger was the artist, the banjo player; his brother was on guitar. It provided me comfort every night. The way I acquired the CD was an act of Spirit...

After answering an ad to work at a factory assembling banjos, I realized being there for the 7:00 a.m. to 3:00 p.m. shift would interfere drastically with the routine that kept me sober. Plus, it was a commute across town during rush hour. I scrapped the idea of working there. Before I left, I was prompted to go into their showroom where the CDs were displayed. The salesman had followed me, so I asked him to recommend something mellow and soothing - nurturing. He picked out Jens Kruger's *The Bridge.* This CD saved me emotionally. I played it not only at night, but also while driving. I let it play and play and play, all the while sucking in the comfort I so desperately sought.

Today, I have thoughts about the significance of this and the role of Spirit in guiding me. I believe I was drawn, or guided, to the factory because I liked blue grass music. As I was a violinist at the time and former guitarist, I enjoyed the various instruments in the ensemble. I appreciated Jens' banjo music because it was not twangy. Rather, it was smooth and flowing - lovely. I discovered his music to be soothing. Spirit connected me with *The Bridge* so I could be comforted.

The point of the banjo story is two-fold. First, you like me, may find it touching and I wanted to share the experience with you as an example of the ways in which Spirit works for all of us. Second, it's an example and a reminder of how you, too, can become alert to and aware of Spirit's presence in all areas of *your* life.

HOPE

I've read that HOPE is an acronym. It stands for Hold On, Pain Ends. In all the years I prayed every night for tomorrow to be better, I had never heard that HOPE was a way to look at pain from another point of view. In my travels, I have learned pain does indeed end. For me, that occurred after I found a way to forgive my past and be grateful for the dock mate debacle.

The length of time pain lasts is directly proportional to your level of willingness to be open to new ideas and suggestions. The more open you are, the more often you choose the way of willingness to heal. When you choose the way of willingness, the more quickly you can move through the healing journey. From my stories, you see that you, too, can hang on through your pain. You now know and hopefully trust, it ends.

HOPE also stands for Hold On, Possibilities Emerge. These possibilities appear as opportunities. Sometimes they are messages from others, sometimes in books, sometimes an offer in person. Actually, they come from all around you. The key is to watch for them and be aware of their presence. Take any recommended course of action the emerging possibility seems to warrant is appropriate.

In my recovery, I discovered that when the pain ended, possibilities appeared - actually emerged. They came to me in words others said and in books, including my meditation books. They especially came from that soft, quiet voice I had come to know as my Divine guide, my inner Spirit. The point is, when possibilities emerge, when opportunities knock consider it is Spirit. Hold out hope all will be well if you let go and trust. I invite you to believe you're being guided in the direction needed for your healing and growth. Take action on the things Spirit whispers quietly again and again.

From HOPE, you can conclude pain will end and new opportunities will make themselves known to you. When they do, I invite you to go beyond any fear you may have. Step in to your courage and move forward. When it's the right thing for you and you've done any necessary work, everything will flow smoothly and fall into place. Doors will open. If it's not right, things won't turn out. You'll encounter door-after-door that is closed. I invite you to cease forcing and to wait for the possibilities to emerge. They will. Be mindful of them. Act.

For many, many years, I prayed, asking that tomorrow be better than today so I could have peace. It was a prayer I'd been saying every night since I was in high school. Although I asked politely and didn't complain, tomorrow came and was often pretty much like today - in other words, difficult. Still, I persevered and held out hope, which is why I love the meanings of the acronym for HOPE; they're both true. And, the peace I sought came after four years of sobriety when I discovered forgiveness.

After much time sober, I realized opportunities had come to me over the years. Some I took, like going to a twelve-step meeting with my roommate. Some I didn't take, mostly because I was not at a point where I could recognize an opportunity was being offered to me. If I did recognize it, I was afraid to follow that path. Instead of being curious about my reluctance, I criticized the path and came up with a myriad of reasons why it was flawed. Ah, typical blaming behavior to avoid failing or looking deficient...

When you have a desire, a dream, or a prayer for something to occur, it becomes much easier to see the resources emerge when you have three attitudes. These attitudes are ones you choose. You recognize opportunities when you choose to see with an:

1. Attitude of curiosity,
2. Openness to new ideas, and
3. Willingness to re-assess your beliefs.

Choice

Choice is *crucial* for a peaceful, free life. You make the decision of what your attitude and mindset are at any given moment in time. You have the freedom to see things from a positive point of view. You can also choose to see things negatively. It all takes energy. Actually, being negative takes more energy. It's all a matter of mindset and how you'd like to experience life - with positives lifting you and others up, or negatives, bringing you and them down.

When people told me this in early sobriety, I wanted to smack them. It made me angry they couldn't see or understand how damaged I was. How could I move forward if that were the case? How could I be positive about the wounds? I learned after many years, my behavior and thought processes were those of a victim. It was Dr. Luskin's three questions that turned my attitude from that of a victim to one of a victor.

During the years I stayed in the marriage, I felt I had no choice but to remain. The fact is I *did* have a choice. I could choose to stay or leave. The reasons I chose to stay are things such as, I was afraid my leaving would devastate him. Besides, we were good party friends; I could continue to party with him. A lot of it, though, was my fear to be alone in the world, single. I did hold love for my husband, yet it faded. We complemented each other well in our skills needed for all the renovation work we performed. However, we worked together poorly. Toward the end, I had little energy to do anything other than continue on as usual.

These were my choices, my reasons for staying, albeit poor ones. As I mentioned before, the choice of staying was a destructive act on my part. I stayed, criticizing and degrading my husband with my control and manipulation. For many years, my defense was, I had behaved as I did in response to *his* verbal and emotional putdowns. Yet at fifteen years sober, about three years ago, I discovered this was true - in part. Some of the truth is I was totally unreasonable in the rules I had set. Furthermore, I was not realistic in what I expected of him. Nonetheless, when he didn't meet my rules and expectations, I lashed out verbally and emotionally. We both did, actually.

My stomach drops as I re-read the two preceding paragraphs. I think back on how I treated him over the years. It's a pang of guilt, tinged with a little shame. Definitely embarrassment and deep sadness because of the unrest I no doubt caused. Did I intend the discord to go on as it did? No! Yet, in the end, it was what it was. The manner in which I chose to leave the marriage was very hurtful, I'm sure. Even though I've forgiven myself, thoughts about how I handled the whole thing bring me sadness.

Here again I have a choice. I can learn from this experience and not treat anyone else that way, or I can perhaps do it again to someone else. I can also wallow in my guilt. The key is to learn. I choose to do just that and not repeat it. I can also choose whether I want to feel guilty about it or not. I did allow myself some guilt, then I moved on to gratitude that I now know this about myself. I can be watchful for bad behavior in the future and nip it in the bud. Finally, I learned the energy I spent today being upset and regretful over yesterday was time wasted. I had better things to do.

Before we go on, I'd like to clarify one point. By looking at my own behavior and calling myself out, I am in no way negating or excusing the verbal and emotional negative treatment I received from my husband. It took its toll. Instead, I am examining my own behavior to see where I might have contributed, in order to learn from it and to improve myself as a person in a future relationship.

As we go deeper into the art of forgiveness, you become more able to notice the choices you are making, when all the while you thought you had no choice. If, for example, you choose to stay in a relationship where verbal, emotional, or physical onslaughts occur, you can choose to succumb to the abuse and tolerate it. Or, you can choose to do what you need to do in the relationship to take care of yourself. Do what you need to do to stay centered and safe. You may wish to join a support group that deals with the specific problem you are experiencing. You may need to leave the relationship.

One of the things I chose to fight over was my husband's habit of staying after work to hang out with the guys. The unspoken rule was I expected him to be at home with me. I'd wait and wait, and become angrier and angrier by the minute. Finding and planning something I could have done when my husband didn't come home right away would have benefited our marriage.

For example, I might have taken an adult education class in an area of my interest. I could have scheduled activities at the end of the workday, such as dinner with a friend, shopping, or a movie. I could have read a book. I think you get the point. I could have engaged in activities that fed my soul. I had no idea there was such a thing - feeding my soul. I also had no idea I was responsible to enrich my life and myself in order to facilitate growth. I'm so happy to know this now. I invite you to explore the ways in which you feed *your* soul, the ways in which you enrich *your* life.

Let's return to HOPE and "Possibilities Emerge." The next thing that occurs for you after the possibilities emerge is opportunities evolve. Brad was a possibility who emerged in my life. His appearance then evolved into an opportunity to heal and grow. If I'd been able to keep the tears at bay, such that he had continued on his way, I would have been mired in my depression and difficulty for much longer than I was. I may not have even come out of it. I probably never would have recognized Brad's attention as the opportunity it was. Over the years, I have repeatedly experienced opportunities being offered to me by Spirit. Today, I know to be grateful for them and to thank that force – even and especially for parking spaces.

I invite you to explore how the issues discussed in this chapter affect you in your life. For example, consider the choices you are making that are forming your journey. Explore the choices you've made. Note how your life changed as a result. Look at the ways in which you are, perhaps, in a situation you don't like, yet, you're choosing to stay. What are your choices and why are you choosing them? Is it fair to all parties? How do you experience HOPE in your life right now? Are you waiting for the pain to end or the possibilities to emerge? Do you have trouble asking for help? If you do, what's behind that? Is it shame, unworthiness? Look closely at these things, with candor, with curiosity - not shame. May you discover the things about yourself to celebrate! They are there, ever emerging, always evolving.

CHAPTER 4

The Art of Forgiveness

"Forgiveness means that even though you're wounded,
You choose to hurt and suffer less."
— Dr. Fred Luskin

The Van

After ten months of walking, writing, and going to meetings throughout the day, I had leftover energy. I didn't know what to do with it. The urge to road trip tugged at me again. This time, I was able to heed the call and make plans to go. In this chapter, you glimpse the creation of a space I prepared and lived in for three years while I voyaged. In addition to describing the van creation, the story of the evolving art of forgiveness continues.

You begin to discover how everything fits together, and you become able to form your own art of forgiveness. In Chapter 6, *Anger, Resentment, and Beyond,* we explore anger you've experienced or experience, and the feelings beneath it. With the knowledge and insight you gain, it is possible for you to put all the pieces together. Thus, you can create your own beautiful work of art.

According to Ms. Casarjian in *Houses of Healing,* your highest Self wants inner peace and freedom. Yet, the ego robs you of freedom by disallowing the sight of and connection to, yours or another's Self. When you don't act from a place of Self and don't connect with another's, you become tired, numb, anxious, in pain, and in chronic anger. Are you able to see another's Self, so you can really connect? Can you see *your*

Self? Or are you, like I was, operating from a non-Self space, not even aware you possessed an adult Self and an inner child? I invite you to write about what thoughts and feelings come up.

On my trip down the coast to my friend's home in Ocean Beach, I found it got old pitching camp every night and then tearing it down in the morning. From this experience, I was leaning toward a camper van of some sort. Having owned a VW bus when I was married, I knew it was a lot easier as a travel vehicle. The deciding point was my dream to cruise in a sailboat. Doing so in my boat had been rudely interrupted. My purchase of a van would be like cruising, only I'd be doing it in a vehicle - on land rather than by sea.

After some searching for one that needed interior work, I found a full-sized, 1984 Dodge van/RV. One of the two bulkhead walls, the walls dividing the sitting/bed area from the closet and the toilet that were in the very rear of the van, had been cut off diagonally. It was the driver's side that was cut. Apparently, this was done so a tall person could sleep along the bench seat.

This van was perfect for me because it needed work I knew how to complete. With the exception of the bulkhead walls that needed to be rebuilt, it was cosmetic and very fixable. The energy and skills I gained from many past renovation projects got put to great use. The knowledge gained during my marriage to a mechanic and electronics wizard also was very useful with the twelve-volt electricity and the water system. The three years I lived and worked on the boat contributed as well.

I dove into the project. To begin with, I gutted the interior except the stove, refrigerator, and sink. The panels of plywood on the walls went away. They served as patterns for new panels that I cut out of cherry plywood. I designed and built two new bulkhead walls separating the sitting/sleeping area from the rear of the van. I replaced the two walls that were there, including the one that had been cut. The passenger side bulkhead wall provided privacy for the porta-potty while the other wall, the driver's side, hid my hanging and folded clothes.

At the top of each wall, I built a shelf. These two shelves were made of plywood covered with cherry veneer. The trim was solid cherry and was - of course - varnished. It reflected like a mirror. My van creation was quite similar to that of a classic boat interior, only with cherry wood instead of teak. I felt like I was living in my very own sailing vessel. It became a nurturing haven for my reading, writing, and cuddling with my twenty-year-old kitty, Maynard. All three were integral to my healing.

The van project lasted four months. It was a *huge* and healthy diversion from my angst about keeping sober. Once completed, Maynard and I set off to travel the Western States and Baja, Mexico. This we did with great gusto and curiosity. We enjoyed new experiences together. Once I built a booster seat for Maynard to sit on, he was quiet while he enjoyed watching the world go by.

When not driving, I read voraciously. I was thirsty for the words, the feelings, the comfort. There were three books that made a huge impression on me: *The Invitation,* by Oriah Mountain Dreamer, *Until Today,* a daily meditation book by Iyanla Vanzant, and *The Power of Now,* by Eckhart Tolle. These books helped me in my quest for spirituality and sanity. I also attended meetings along the way and journaled every day. At night and while driving, I listened to *The Bridge.*

At the end of three years in the van, Maynard died; I grieved for many months before I could bear to get a new kitty. Soon after his death, my adventure ended. I moved into an apartment in order to recover from an upcoming wrist reconstruction surgery. After surgery and a year of rehab, I stepped into the entrepreneurial world. First, I photographed and sold fine art images of wrought iron gates. Next I published a book of these images, paired with inspirational verses I'd written. Recently this book, *Opening the Gates of the Heart*, won a silver medal for world peace in the 2018 Living Now Evergreen Book Awards. What an honor!

Six years ago, I started studying in preparation to become a motivational speaker and forgiveness mentor. For three years I read books on forgiveness, gratitude, trauma, and anger, took speaking classes, became an award-winning Toastmaster, and obtained certification as a life coach. I began speaking and coaching three years ago about how to create forgiveness in one's life. Throughout all of this, my years as a practicing nurse were useful in that the compassion and empathy I felt then and now were/are second nature to me. Additionally, my years at the State job benefited me in the ability to develop programs and workshops. This program, I learned from a person who contracts with the State, is still being used today.

It was within this framework and mindset that I began to unconsciously establish the art of forgiveness. The stages I went through on my journey to peace and freedom are reflected in the pages of my gates book. Years later, when I started creating workshops, I used as a model those stages from the book. After all, I was a living example of someone who had gone through them and had been successful in learning to forgive. The way in which this process came to life was and is special...

Accidental Forgiveness

Dr. Jim Dincalci, the author of *How to Forgive When You*

Can't, says it's possible to heal a lifetime of anger, blame, resentment, grudges, and especially regret, guilt, and self-blame, so you can enjoy more peace and joy in your life. When I read this, the words rang true for me. My own experiences with anger proved him correct. As I recalled my angry times, I remembered how miserable I was inside. Yet, when I healed my grief and the feelings under my anger, the misery resolved itself.

What *initially* catapulted me to peace and freedom was when I discovered how to forgive my past. This discovery of forgiveness led me to let go of my anger, blame, and resentment. The regret, guilt, and self-blame were resolved years later when I forgave myself. It brought me to the peace and joy about which Dr. Dincalci writes.

Using my experiences and newly found knowledge from reading and researching, I created the forgiveness programs I now share with clients and audiences. I named the process I experienced myself, the "art of forgiveness." To guide you through making your *own* art of forgiveness, I created the *YIPPEE Method.* It's the nuts and bolts of the art of forgiveness. The *YIPPEE Method* has six stages you experience; they are defined later in this chapter and thoroughly in Chapter 5. This brings us to my discovery of forgiveness. It was actually quite by accident. It happened because of the healing journey I was pursuing…

In 2004, I made it back to Marin County to show off my three-year-old sobriety to my drinking buddies. I decided they weren't so "out there" after all. One day I found it difficult to be around people when they were drinking, so decided to go on a mini-adventure to a campground outside of town. On the very first morning of my sojourn, it was bright and sunny. I sat at the table in the van, drinking my ever-present coffee and journaling. It was on this day I stumbled upon a way to forgive my past.

There I was, poised to journal, when the bright idea came to me to do a self-appraisal. I had conducted two or three of them prior to the idea. *This* time, however, I would look specifically at the ways in which *my* behavior had led to the demise of the close relationships I'd had with men over the course of my life. What I quickly realized was, I used to get drunk, and yell and scream at them they were *worthless*, and would never amount to *anything*. Oh my goodness! My horror and guilt were *huge!* I'm grateful they've each forgiven me!

What I focused on, though, was the fact that I didn't even *mean* it about them. I meant it about *myself!* Whoa. This was an aha! moment. Suddenly, I had an epiphany! It stood to reason, and it was logical, that *all those years* I was told I was worthless and would never amount to anything, the person who told me this really meant it about himself/herself, not about me.

This was *profoundly* life changing! In that instant, I saw this person as a fellow human being who was wounded, just like me. I felt compassion for him/her. After all, I knew how the worthless wound felt. Over the period of a year, I kept going back and forth between anger and compassion - anger over what had happened and compassion because I felt the pain of my offender's wound in addition to mine. One day, I suddenly realized I had forgiven the offender, forgiven my past. I had opened up a space in my heart using compassion, and forgiveness had flowed into the space I'd created.

I can't *tell* you how peaceful and freeing that feeling of forgiveness was and is! I *can* tell you it was immediate and *immense!* This realization allowed me to further develop my abilities to offer compassion and empathy. In current day, I continue to feel these emotions for wounds someone might have endured. I know how awful it feels to be wounded and in pain.

Let me point out something. All those years of resentment, I was taking the offense of my offender too personally. The issue is the offense had nothing to *do* with me. The offender was merely trying to handle his/her own pain, his/her own wound. He/she was hurting and took it out on me. These points are not said to condone what was done; what happened was not okay. Even so, the offender taking it out on me is an indicator he/she was wounded. Now I realize this, it is possible to gain compassion, or at least the beginning of it, more quickly.

I believe when one human hurts or kills another being, the inflictor of pain is wounded underneath all the angst and anguish. Dr. Sandra Wilson states in her book *Hurt People Hurt People*, we are surrounded by people who hurt each other. They do so because of the "... seemingly inescapable pain in their own lives." One thing you learn from Dr. Wilson's book is people hurt others in the same ways they have been hurt. As a result of considering this, my experience confirms you do begin to see your offender differently. You realize what he/she went through himself/herself. You see with more compassion and understanding, more empathy.

After this occurs, you learn to be aware of and alert to possibilities that will present themselves to further your understanding of the offender's wounds. This allows you to generate more compassion and empathy. Knowing these things are going to occur aids you to be alert for them. Most importantly, know these two practices are the precursors to forgiveness. When utilized, they hasten your ability to forgive.

You don't forget the offense that started your anger, your resentment. That's not how it works. The offense is a part of your being, a part of who you are. The only way to forget it is to stuff it deep inside; even then, it affects your every move. Instead of forgetting, you see your hurt and the offender with a softer heart. When you recognize and acknowledge your offender's hurt, you begin to make room for forgiveness to enter. You begin to allow it to flow into the empty space you now know you can create in your heart by your practices of compassion and empathy. This allows you to let go of your anger, which cannot exist in the presence of compassion, empathy, and forgiveness.

The YIPPEE Method

I used the acronym *YIPPEE* in order that you can exclaim, "Yippee! I'm going to find peace and freedom from my resentment!" It is in this declaration that you exhibit the beginnings of willingness. Willingness is the key - it drives everything.

Composed of six stages, *YIPPEE* is an acronym. It stands for Yearn, Investigate, Process, Practice, Evolve, and Empower. Each stage has within it certain actions, beliefs, and/or behaviors to achieve before proceeding to the next stage. This is all detailed in Chapter 5, *The YIPPEE Method*. It is within the *Empower* stage that forgiveness gently appears and begins to fill a space in your heart you created in the *Evolve* stage when you learned to hold the offender in your heart with compassion and empathy.

While I was developing the *YIPPEE Method*, I came to the realization that all the ups and downs of my journey - the healing and growth I'd done - were the nuts and bolts of the art of forgiveness. Said differently, within the art of forgiveness lies the *YIPPEE Method*. This art form is a two-steps-forward-one-step-back kind of dance, in that you make gains, and you experience setbacks and roadblocks. That's because you're dealing with your own emotions, as well as the feelings of others. These fluctuate and can be difficult to manage. Maintaining gratitude helps.

You're a human being and are designed to make mistakes so you can learn from them and then teach others. You, as well as all of us, have a light and a dark side. The point is, you occasionally do mean things or say something offensive to others. You do the same to yourself. This happens in the course of living, yet, it can change. The key is to first identify and then develop willingness to explore why you did or said what you did so you can determine what you were feeling at the time. Once you assess the entire situation, you come to a decision of how to handle it. You then choose the action(s) needed to reach your desired outcome.

I discovered something amazing about setbacks and roadblocks. Many of them were of my own making! Furthermore, I learned I was *choosing* thoughts, behaviors, and actions that were leading to the setbacks. Hmmm. I began to identify and assess the choices I was unconsciously making. Being able to be conscious of choices occurred for me somewhere along the way as I created the art of forgiveness. This awareness that I had a choice was *not* something I had developed during my drinking years; knowing about it was new to me and special. Becoming able to be conscious of *your* choices is an important part of the journey.

Certainly, the fact I'd embarked upon sobriety was the driving force allowing me to take this journey at all. As a drinker, I would have continued to resent and blame everyone and everything for my misery. This is what we did, we drinkers. I was darn good at it. I wallowed in resentment and blame for my husband and everyone else for various reasons. As I write and reflect upon this, thinking of the wallowing exhausts me, drags me down, and leaves me feeling sad, rather than feeling happy and joyous with renewed energy. Imagine how entrenched I was in my negativity, in the weights dragging me down. It's the backpack thing, filled with rocks that, in the instant of self-reflection when I reached forgiveness, fell out of the pack.

It never occurred to me to look at my own behavior in any given situation. I had no experience with or concept of being accountable or responsible for my feelings. I was responsible for my actions – mostly, my feelings - no. Alcohol prevented me from looking. Now, having ceased drinking and blaming - for the most part - I look within first. As a result, I have discovered the kind and loving woman inside. I've also seen the bad behavior I exhibit at times. Even so, I am much lighter and have more energy. This is because when you are able to consider your words and actions, you catch your unkind and unloving behaviors. Letting go of them is freeing. You gain physical lightness and energy when you do. It's the backpack emptying…

It took some years of healing and growing to accept responsibility for my feelings. It was so engrained in me to blame, to look at everyone else as the problem. Additionally, it was the preferred method of avoiding responsibility practiced by this alcoholic and many others. It took some time to remember to look at myself before I looked at anyone else. When I did, amazing revelations occurred that led, and lead, me to treat others and myself with more love and kindness. For example, in the past three or four years, I discovered I was subtly still blaming an offender for past hurts, even though I'd forgiven that person. Realizing this caught me off guard. I had no idea how deep the need and urge to blame ran.

The realization of how far-reaching my blaming was, occurred when I heard a friend and colleague say something that got my attention. She referenced the way in which she blamed her offenders for her present day feelings, rather than totally owning them. She would not let him/her off the hook, and kept calling out or "outing" her offender. My colleague stated that by "outing" him/her, she was trying to shame, to punish. Her current belief was she needed to be totally responsible for what she was feeling in present day, without mentioning, without "outing" her offender.

The shock to realize how I so subtly still blamed, that I even *continued* to do it, hit me in the gut like a two-by-four. Wow! You see I was doing just what my friend and colleague described. I was outing my offender when I made speeches, when I told my story. I was calling that person out. I was making the events and the hurt more important than the lessons and gratitudes. Even though I was not aware of it, this hindered the depth at which I could heal and experience forgiveness.

Although I knew I'd forgiven my offender, I realized after I discovered I was "outing" this person, I still needed to heal at a deeper level. I needed to look at the hurt and consider what I was getting out of it when I "outed" him/her. Aha!

What I discovered was, I still wanted to punish. This is rather embarrassing to say, yet, I want you to understand the things to examine when your embarrassing behaviors and beliefs pop up. As a result of my realizing I was out to make him/her feel badly, I once again renewed my compassion and empathy at a deeper level.

By examining what I was getting out of it, I was able to stop "outing" the offender and tell my story differently, as my level of forgiveness had deepened. I became more grateful and that led to more empowerment. Additionally, exploring my behavior with you instead of hiding it due to embarrassment took away the power this embarrassing admission had over me.

I invite you to consider forgiveness in your life. Are you willing to consider forgiving? That's where it starts. "No!" you exclaim. "I will *not* condone what was done to me." Ah, that's not what forgiveness teaches. It teaches the offender is held responsible for his/her actions. Forgiving him/her does not mean you overlook what was done. You are not condoning the offense. You are merely clearing your own heart, your own soul. You are healing and getting beyond the resentment for yourself, not for anyone else. It has nothing to do with the offender. You're just trying to set yourself free of the bond you have with blame and anger toward the person you resent.

Before going to the *YIPPEE Method*, I invite you to write down one person whom you would like to forgive. What prevents you from forgiving him/her? Now write down one thing about yourself that you need to forgive. What stops you from forgiving yourself? Hold these thoughts. You'll learn to process them in the next chapter.

When I started thinking back on how I'd gained the ability to forgive, how I'd struggled to get to that point, I realized what I'd experienced might be of use to others, to you. After all, I got beyond a *huge* bitter resentment - all with forgiveness and the actions and revelations preceding its discovery. This is how the *YIPPEE Method* was born. Come with me to the next chapter; let me introduce it...

CHAPTER 5

The YIPPEE Method

"The human soul does not want to be
Advised, fixed, or saved.
It simply wants to be witnessed… exactly as it is."

Parker Palmer

The *YIPPEE Method* is a system, a process, that when worked through, brings a smile to your face and peace to your heart and soul. I created it in response to the need to get from a point of resentment and unrest to a place of peace and freedom. The end result is forgiveness. It is the process I have described in this book about my story from devastation and anger to that forgiving place. *YIPPEE* is an acronym that stands for Yearn, Investigate, Process, Practice, Evolve, and Empower. In this chapter, the *Method* is explored in the hopes it resonates with you, such that you find it useful for your journey.

"Y" Stands for Yearn

In the course of my life, I learned all the reasons why I *should* hold on to the anger I created when I was wronged. "What happened is the *truth*," I'd say. "And this is what it *did* to me." I could not let this go. I was fifty-five and seven years sober when I started wanting even more deeply to experience peace and freedom from the resentment instead of the anger and bitterness, the seething and chaos. I was *yearning* for peace of mind, freedom from resentment. You may recognize yourself in these words. Perhaps, you want to get rid of anger and resentment in *your* life. The answer is to yearn for peace, for freedom, and to want it more than the anger. That's the point of the *Yearn* stage. Let's explore it…

Willingness

It all starts with willingness. This is the first of four points in the *Yearn* stage. Having willingness is the key to everything. When you are willing to listen to new ideas and concepts, and incorporate them into your life, you are on the right track. When you are willing to look at yourself, to examine your kind and loving, as well as your unkind, unloving, or mean behavior - and accept responsibility - you are on your way. You increase your chances of coming to forgiveness more quickly. If you are willing to consider forgiving, you are embarking upon a tremendously beautiful experience.

The key to the process of forgiveness, according to Ms. Casarjian of *Houses of Healing*, is gaining the willingness to "see," to be Self-aware. When you "see" the Self in others and "see" *your* Self, your adult Self, you become empowered. You become free from getting tangled in judgments of others *and* yourself. You have the power that prevents others from upsetting you.

I invite you to develop willingness to look at, notice, and consider anything and everything that comes across your path. Develop awareness for your physical surroundings. Notice and consider those you meet during the day. Be curious about their plight. By doing this, you develop the habit of willingness and, through habit, become willing to look at yourself also. Learning and developing the ability to live with willingness is crucial. You'll need it in order to perform the exploration of self that occurs in this *YIPPEE Method*. It's a skill that develops with practice. I invite you to be encouraged you are gaining what you are gaining in each present moment. Be grateful for the level at which you currently identify issues of growth for yourself. Know your skill and healing abilities will grow.

One thing you could do is ask yourself, "What are new experiences I can have on this day, in this moment, that add to my growth, my richness of life?" When you have the willingness to view life in such a manner, your chances of reaching that point of growth and richness improve. Thus, your chances of finding forgiveness and the resulting peace and freedom are that much greater.

Perform willingness checks throughout the day that confirm or deny the level at which you are operating. Pose questions to yourself and rate them on a scale of one to ten, with ten being very willing, and one being not willing at all. A sample question to ask might be, "How willing am I to conduct random willingness checks on myself throughout the day?" If you rate yourself eight or less on the scale, write about what's behind your reluctance, your resistance.

Letting Go/Surrender

As you yearn, the second point to consider is letting go or surrendering. According to Dr. Luskin in *Forgive for Good*, it takes willingness to let go of three things. Once you learn to let these things go, you experience more peace. On the other hand, when you are unable or unwilling to let them go, you will likely find yourself resenting someone or yourself. I invite you to consider the three things. They are *hugely* important to explore. Learn to let go of...

1. The need to be right,
2. The need to have your own way, and
3. The need to control other people and situations.

Let's explore the need to be right. This starts *many, many* arguments. Think of this situation as an example: Two people each have their opinion about something. Each person believes he/she is right and will not even *consider*, let alone *listen* to, the other person's opinions, beliefs, or feelings. Each has shut down and is unwilling to open his/her heart and mind. As a result, all communications and opportunities to resolve differences are shattered. Even the ability to have tolerance for the other is severed.

To avoid this, I invite you to respectfully listen to another's thoughts before you relay yours. Practice tolerance and patience. If it's safe and not abusive, stay, ask questions, and really listen. On the other hand, if you are unsafe or being abused in any way, leave if you can - even to another room - and seek help. It does no good to try to get the other to consider your points if he/she is being abusive.

As you listen to the other, try not to formulate the response in your mind as he/she is talking. Let it be about them, not about you. Instead, listen. Try to put yourself in the other's shoes. Allow him/her to finish thoughts. Many times, people become angry when they're not being acknowledged or they get interrupted before they finish their comment. To provide a safe and respectful space for this person, it is necessary to allow him/her to finish despite opposition you may feel toward what he/she is saying. You may be pulled to speak up with your own point. Instead, be still and silent.

When it's your turn to speak, avoid a loud or angry stance or tone of voice. Be curious. If the difference in opinion is proven by fact to which you have access, state it rationally with the evidence that demonstrates the fact. If the other person starts to argue, remember: It takes two to fight. I invite you to back off. Keep the knowledge of the facts without smugness or an attitude of "I'm right and you're wrong." That mindset pits you against the other and is toxic. Gain peace from the knowledge that the facts are correct.

The next time you feel the urge to get in an argument to prove you're right, stop yourself. Let go of worrying about the other person's lack of desire or ability to understand facts. Become aware of gloating; let it go if you're doing this. Take a deep breath and remember: Sometimes it's futile to try and get others to listen to your opinion or even facts. After all, they are just as firm on the belief of their "rightness" as you are on yours. Let go, respect their freedom of choice, and gain peace. Be at peace with your knowledge and try not to force the other person to see it your way.

Let's consider the need to have your own way. When you have such a need, it sets up a resentment, as you expect the experience to look like "this." When it looks like "that," you might get upset, even angry. Underneath that anger is likely disappointment. There may be other feelings as well, such as hurt, humiliation, or shame. Remember to look for feelings underneath the anger. Remember also, an unrealistic expectation is a resentment waiting to happen. Sometimes, when we don't get our way, we withhold love and affection from our loved ones. Do you do this? Look closely. Give them your love and attention instead.

How do you respond when you don't get your way? Look at one behavior in which you engage when you're disappointed or angry that things didn't turn out the way you'd like. I invite you to examine that behavior, even if it brings embarrassment. This mindset of embarrassment can be explored and changed if you choose. By considering with curiosity the feelings underneath your anger and resentment, you begin to get beyond them as they are acknowledged, felt, and resolved. You gain empowerment when this happens.

As far as controlling others and situations? It is *futile!* There is no point using your time and energy in this way. Forcing the other person leads to resentment from them. Others cannot be controlled, as much as we'd like to do it sometimes. Rather than trying to manage and control others or situations, I invite you to focus on *your* behavior and actions. If these need adjusting, make the necessary changes. Practice excitement for the unknown that will occur as the day progresses. Be grateful.

Focusing on yourself and not others can be said another way that's rather blunt and almost rude. Here it is: Draw a three-foot-diameter circle around yourself. This is your space. Your *only* business is everything *inside* the circle. Whatever is outside is *not* your business. Try not to get yourself involved in others' business or affairs. Rather than trying to change others to fit into what you desire, I invite you to focus on learning to appreciate them for who and what they are, giving them space to be exactly that - themselves. Discover and know another's value does not diminish your own. Allowing others to express who they are, is a wonderful way to show respect while you acknowledge them as a being, a Self.

Acceptance

The third of the four points in the *Yearn* stage is to gain and practice acceptance. If there is something in your life that is disturbing and you can take some action to deal with it to alter the situation, do so. Determine your feelings and how they led to your situation. However, if there's nothing you can do, accept it. It is not productive and not a good use of time and energy to keep lamenting over the roadblock. Examine it, accept it, and look forward to new possibilities that are emerging, new opportunities that are coming to you. This establishes a positive energy that attracts more positivity and opportunity.

If something is meant to be, it will work out easily, without force. Doors will open. On the other hand, if it's not the right thing for you, doors will close and you'll be butting your head against that door. Rather than repeatedly bruising your head, accept the situation and move forward with excitement for what's to come.

Gratitude

Gratitude can trans*form* your life. It is the fourth and final point in the *Yearn* stage. Actually, gratitude allows you to *transcend* your difficulty! That's right. You can rise above it *permanently* when you're a grateful person. Once you display gratitude, more positive experiences come to you for which you are grateful, and this positivity attracts more things that fill you with gratitude. This generates additional positive experiences, and so forth. It's a never-ending upward spiral of gratitude and positivity.

Through his three questions discussed in Chapter 1, Dr. Luskin provides an excellent way to achieve gratitude. Furthermore, I discovered these questions worked well with a variety of emotions. For me, his questions worked on my feelings of failure, regret, self-hatred, and grief. I guess, with the exception of grief, these are all examples of self-resentment, now aren't they? That's why the questions worked so well! As a refresher, here they are. Ask and answer them about resentment, anger or other feelings.

1. What is the lesson(s) I learned or am learning from the situation?
2. What is the positive that is resulting or resulted because of it?
3. What can I be grateful for?

I had great difficulty adopting gratitude in sobriety. It angered me that being grateful was frequently the topic of the meetings I attended. *"What??? Gratitude again???"* I'd exclaim angrily. "I'm so *sick* of gratitude. Can't they find something *else* to talk about?" My former roommate, who is reading the book, relayed to me that as she was reading this chapter, she remembers us rolling our eyes at each other when gratitude was called as a topic. That's right! Those were the days when gratitude was a weight around my being. It was difficult to hear about it, as I was so wounded and hurt, and couldn't appreciate *anything* about my life. Listening to another's reasons for being grateful was excruciating. I wonder if my old roommate felt the same way...

As I write this, I give a deep sigh of relief. I recognize what I describe was worlds ago. Life has certainly changed. When this journey of healing began, I thought I would never feel good. I felt I would never be at peace inside or with the world around me. Enough has taken place over the years such that I am now bathed in peace and gratitude. I say this in the spirit of encouragement. While you may feel you'll stay in an emotion forever, you won't, trust me. Keep looking forward with gratitude. Things change. Focus on finding gratitudes.

Truly, if you practice gratitude, compassion, and forgiveness, time will pass more quickly and be more pleasant. If you are stuck in a thought pattern in which you feel you'll always be weighed down by your bad feelings, remember HOPE: Hold On, Pain Ends. You can make it end more quickly if you practice being grateful, as well as offering compassion and forgiveness to another.

Another thing to consider is this: focus on the things in front of you, the next right thing to do, and then do it - again and again and again. Focus on self-awareness and openness. Doing these things will help you resolve pain more quickly.

If gratitude is an attitude you'd like to adopt and practice, yet, you can't seem to get going on it, I have a suggestion. I invite you to start a gratitude journal. Here's what to do: Each morning as you do your wake up routine, take time to write down one thing for which you are grateful. Explain *why* you feel this gratitude. Then thank Spirit, or whatever you choose to be your spirit of power.

If you don't believe in a force greater than yourself, just say thank you into the air. This gratitude attracts positivity and more gratitudes. Do this writing exercise every morning for twenty-one days. Keep with it. After this time, it becomes a habit. You will notice a change in your ability to carry gratitude with you throughout the day. When you do this, you begin to live in a state of grace.

At the end of this stage, the *Yearn* stage, you can experience an uplifting of spirit and the beginnings of a mindset shift. You may have gained gratitude for things bothering you and this changes your perception, allowing you to be more positive.

Let's move to the second stage, the "I" stage.

"I" Stands for Investigate

In this stage, your task is to list on paper up to five grievances against another or yourself. By "grievances," I mean both anger and/or resentment. Choose one grievance to explore and set the list aside for later reference. For the grievance you chose, list your current feelings associated with it. This could include disappointment, hurt, shame, humiliation, loss or anticipation of loss, regret, guilt, and/or remorse. Just list them. You'll work through the entire process on each grievance one at a time through to the end. Please know it's not as overwhelming as it sounds.

I invite you to be entirely present for this exploration without imbibing in substances that alter your consciousness. You'll appreciate the clarity you gain as a result. As you review the one grievance you listed and chose to work through, allow difficult feelings to surface, and as they do, be still. Allow them to float through your mind without fighting them, without judgment, anger, shame, regret, or feelings of worthlessness. Identify them, while knowing they will pass through your mind shortly after arriving. Be still. You can achieve this same state if you meditate, as Dr. Golden and other experts advocate. Once the difficult feelings leave, write in your journal about the experience, including listing the feelings you felt. When your list is complete, proceed to the *Process* stage. A word of caution: Only work one resentment at a time through to the end of the *YIPPEE Method*.

The *Investigate* stage can be difficult due to the nature of your feelings that likely surface. For those of you who want to get comfortable with a glass of wine to do this exercise, I invite you to become familiar with and to heed Ms. Casarjian's theory. In *Houses of Healing*, she discusses that when you drink, you are at risk of abandoning both your inner, adult Self and your inner child.

She goes on to explain, when you abandon them, you then recreate and play out the offense done to you originally. By doing so, you close yourself off to valuable information that aids in the art of forgiveness. Has this happened for you? Do you feel a separation from your adult Self or your inner child at times? Write with your "other" hand about this. Look more closely at what you're feeling if this separation is occurring for you.

The goal of this stage is met when you've selected one of your five listed grievances and listed your feelings about the offense. When this is complete, go on to the first "P" stage.

"P" Stands for Process

The *Process* stage contains two specific writing exercises, followed by talking to another. As you write, I again invite you to use your "other" hand to allow your deep feelings to surface and clear more quickly. By "other," I mean your non-dominant hand. Printing is easiest. In fact, I've heard even if it's not legible, it will still prompt deep thoughts and feelings to arise. You may wish to write with your dominant hand to capture on paper what you experienced while writing with your other hand.

Now it's time to process the feelings associated with your resentment. Move through this stage with intention and focus, so as not to get caught lingering too long in difficult feelings. The goal of this stage is to recollect the offense so as to explore your resentment without becoming embroiled in negativity and toxicity. Part of the goal includes acknowledging the hurt both your Self and your inner child endured, and then offering support and comfort to each.

Start with the resentment on which you've been working. You're invited to explore it in the first writing exercise. Get ready to time yourself for three minutes. As you prepare to write, this may seem too brief, yet, the limited amount of time assists to keep you focused on the task. It permits you to do the exercise without getting caught up in describing the whole story of your resentment.

Exercise 1, Part 1: Once you have identified your grievance, write in the first person about that specific situation. Use "I" statements. Briefly explore things such as what happened, how it started, how you felt then and now, what you thought of yourself then and now, and one way it affects you in current day. Let it flow. It helps to be brief, rather than elaborating on each point. Stop after three minutes even if you're not done. You can finish later. Get set for the second part of the exercise.

Exercise 1, Part 2: Write again about the offense. This time, write in the third person, as an observer. Use "he/she" statements. Become a private investigator as you consider the incident. Write just the facts as you observed them. What happened and to whom? Be curious, looking without judgment or ridicule. Again, write for three minutes. This portion of the exercise allows you to become detached from your angst, thus, allowing you the flexibility to examine it without getting caught up in the negativity. After you do this part of the exercise, consider whether you are now looking at your resentment from a new perspective.

Exercise 1, Part 3: The last part of this exercise is to write in three minutes your answer to the question, "Does this anger/resentment/feeling still serve me?" If it does still serve you, examine the why of that response. Is it appropriate for your current situation, for example? Also if it still serves you, determine whether you are willing to consider letting go of the resentment and choosing peace and freedom, or whether you need to hang on to it right now. If it *doesn't* serve you any longer, what is your plan for changing your story? Whichever way you decide, determine if you need to perform any tasks. Complete them.

Exercise 2: The second exercise to use to help resolve the anger and resentment you identified is to ask and answer Dr. Luskin's questions. Take three minutes to ask and answer: What is the lesson I'm learning as a result of my resentment? What are the positives occurring because of the situation? What am I grateful for? This is a powerful exercise, as is Exercise 1. In combination, you receive a clear picture of your grievance and what it's all about. You can express your feelings more easily. Most importantly, perhaps, is the change in attitude you experience when you complete both.

To end the *Process* stage for this grievance, choose someone you trust in whom to confide, such as a spiritual advisor, clergy, sponsor, or trusted friend. Talk over what you discovered in your exploration and your writing. Be sure he/she is not going to engage in judging, belittling, criticizing, or ridiculing what you said or wrote. Assure he/she will not repeat to others what you divulge. Speak with this person to minimize the negative self-talk and self-destructive responses that may have surfaced once you listed your feelings.

As you recalled a grievance, you may have easily identified the offender(s) who cruelly hurt you. This brings up two words of caution I'd like to convey, both from Dr. Luskin. First, he warns to be cautious about giving your power away to someone who was cruel to you. In *Forgive for Good*, he says, "There is great danger in giving people without your best interests in mind power over you. There is great danger in giving people who have hurt you power over the way you feel." According to him, an example of giving up your power is staying tied to your offender by blaming him/her for your failures and anger. Is that something you really want to do? Instead, honestly assess if there is value in remaining attached to this anger and resentment. Does it still serve you to be connected to it?

The second thing he cautions is to avoid spending *too* much time focusing on your wounds; it is to your detriment. When you dwell on them, it gives them power over you. They bring you down and it becomes a habit to always be down. Instead, he recommends you spend your time and energy contemplating the benefits of forgiveness versus the negatives of your wounds.

Dr. Luskin tells us we need to acknowledge feelings, yet, not to stay in the old wounds for too long. Ms. Casarjian and Dr. Dincalci also tell us it's important to examine them. Ms. Casarjian claims it's necessary to go back to your inner child to acknowledge the old hurts. Otherwise, the old feelings continue to taint present day. Dr. Dincalci states, "...avoiding your memories is not really in your best interest because this upset remains just under the surface of your awareness, negatively coloring your life."

This activity - the exploration of wounds - was what I had to do prior to gaining forgiveness. In my situation, I had to get somewhat clear on my feelings before I could proceed. When I got to the point of considering self-forgiveness though, I was able to recognize my inner child's hurts and wounds. I felt it necessary to get beyond them as, even in sobriety, things in my heart and mind were negatively affecting my life and my ability to succeed in my business. Even so, the negativity was not as severe as when I drank. Most of the time when I was drinking, I shared my misery ad nauseam. It got to be a habit that, as Dr. Luskin indicates in his book, got me nowhere.

Today if confronted with difficult feelings, I know what to do. I know how to access them, how to prevent becoming morose or stuck. I understand when I get clarification of what I'm feeling, it is extremely helpful to begin to dissipate the resentment and difficult emotions by exploring what's going on with me. After this happens, it is possible to turn my attention back to the art I was creating and complete the *YIPPEE Method*. This *Method* for healing is designed for use over and over again.

It becomes a fine line to determine if you are, in fact, spending too much time writing and contemplating your wounds. If you find yourself getting overly sad or distraught, remind yourself you are looking with compassionate eyes and heart, with curiosity. Allow yourself to question how the feeling or situation for which you hold sadness still serves you. Identify a gratitude you feel over your discoveries. Take a break and find something in the present you can appreciate. Move. Take a walk. Resume your exploration when you feel re-centered.

The task of looking at yourself can be daunting and terrifying. This is what happened with me. I was terrified I'd not find anything of substance, just negatives. In fact, when I did my first appraisal looking at myself, all I could list were the negatives; there were two notebook pages filled with the ways in which I was a crumb on the earth. You may experience something similar; yet, you can get out of that mindset by doing the self-appraisal I defined earlier. Especially take time with listing loving and kind things you did for others and yourself.

Let's take a look at questions to pose about your resentment. Are the feelings you had when you first endured the offense the same feelings you have today? If so, you know how to manage the feelings of Self. After you do, you are able to guide your inner child to resolve any feelings he/she may have by providing comfort and assuring safety.

These exercises promote healing. I'd like to stress that integral with writing and healing is talking with another person about what you discovered. Such a discussion is crucial for the success of the *Process* stage. That's because the effect of what you learned is strengthened when you speak to someone who is safe and trustworthy in whom to confide what you uncovered. As stated earlier, this can help to heal the wound, as well as minimize self-deprecation. Furthermore, when you talk to someone not involved in the situation, you may get an objective point of view, if you ask for one.

Another valuable and necessary activity is moving your body. That is because our toxic experiences stay in the cells of our bodies until we work them out. Whether it is dance, exercise as basic as walking, yoga, or other stretching exercises, it is very important to move your body during this whole process of examining yourself.

Now that you have processed your resentment, set it aside. Let's move on to the second *"P"* stage...

"P" Stands for Practice

Review everything you have experienced up to this point - willingness, letting go, acceptance, gratitude, defining your resentment and resultant feelings, and determining if holding the feelings from your wound still works for you. Be sure to speak to a trusted person or clergy about what came up for you. Be sure to institute regular exercise while you are focusing on self-exploration. These are all the things to keep practicing as often as possible. Develop awareness to remember to do this.

A reminder, as it's so important: I invite you to conduct random willingness checks throughout the day. How willing are you to behave differently to others and yourself by learning to forgive, or to let go? Rate your willingness on this very question from one through ten, with ten being very willing and one being not willing at all. Just as in the other example, if you score an eight or below on the scale, take a look at the feelings that are preventing your willingness to make changes to your behavior. Maybe you are fearful of changing. Explore your fear. Write this exercise with your "other" hand. If you weren't too willing, list how you might become more so. Ideas will arise. Having said that, it's time to explore the first "E" stage.

"E" Stands for Evolve

Increasing your kind and loving treatment of others and yourself is the purpose of this stage. Evolving is about a way to become aware of and strengthen your Self as a being. Behaviors to develop contribute richness to the piece of artwork you are creating. These include such things as kindness, love, tolerance, gentleness, and respect for others' beliefs, cultures, and customs. It also includes the ways in which you talk to people. Be aware of it so you can be as kind and respectful of others as possible. When practicing the things I suggested, be sure to include yourself as a recipient of those very behaviors. Do you practice them on a routine basis? For yourself? For others? If not, write about what's in your way.

Compassion and empathy play a huge role in the forgiveness process and in the whole piece of artwork. They are the desired results for this stage. It was my compassionate and empathetic mindset that led me to forgive my offender. After my mind felt it, I felt it in my heart. The same can be true for you. If you are unable to feel compassion or empathy for your offender, consider how you would feel if the roles were reversed, if the situation that happened to them was happening to you. How might you feel? Would you be hurt, humiliated, shamed?

Once you get a sense of how you might feel in a similar situation, you can develop a desire to offer comfort or words of healing to the other person. See him/her with your heart, as you would see yourself, and you can experience compassion and empathy. Furthermore, assess whether or not you have done what you are resenting. Have you inadvertently offended in the same manner? If so, recognize the offender is a fallible human being, as are you. Offer forgiveness.

In this stage, you complete a self-appraisal, the same one described earlier. As a refresher, and because I added a couple of steps, here's how it goes: List in your journal four kind and loving things you did in the last three days - two for another and two for yourself. Pause. Put down your pen. Reflect upon the fact that you performed these kind and loving acts for others and yourself. This is who you are as a being. At your core, you are kind and loving. Allow yourself to experience the awe and wonder of this statement. Recognize that your kind and loving actions indicate the caring, considerate person that is you.

Keep this thought in your mind until you feel comfortable, until you no longer wish to brush away recognition of your goodness. When you feel a deep knowingness of whom you really are, look at the other side of the coin. List two unkind, unloving, and mean things you did to another and two you did to yourself, all in the past three days. Know these behaviors do not detract from the miracle you are. For these things you've listed, explore what the wound was/is under your words or actions. Show your Self and your inner child compassion for those wounds. Comfort yourself and your child with gentle, soothing words. If needed, apologize to yourself, your inner child, or another. These steps do not excuse your behavior; rather, they are a means of learning so you can grow emotionally.

Normally to close the *Evolve* stage, I share the story of how I found forgiveness. It is the same story I told in the previous chapter. In my experience of telling it, my tale catches people by surprise and, yet, they become able to consider forgiving. Or, they actually do forgive someone when they hear the story.

Before we move on, assess your ability to practice love, kindness, tolerance, respect, consideration, and patience for others. I invite you to consider your offender with compassion and empathy. These things lead to forgiveness.

Join me and explore how to become empowered from the next stage…

"E" Stands for Empower

This stage is all about engaging in behavior and thought processes that lead you to further healing and greater empowerment. It likely was incredibly powerful to perform a self-appraisal. Hopefully, you began to see yourself at your core, to see the wondrous essence of who you are as a being. On the flip side, you became able to see when you acted poorly and you know *why* you acted that way. You determined if a change was needed and chose to make it. This is empowering.

Even so, the *most* empowering part of the art you are creating is finding out how to forgive yourself and others. That is the goal of this stage. Perhaps, it will occur for you as it did for me - naturally, after applying compassion and empathy. Maybe it will occur in a different manner, yet, the result can be the same - immediate and immense feelings of peace and freedom. It may occur as soon as you feel compassion and empathy for your offender, or, it may take some time, like with me. Just relax and let your piece of artwork take shape. Keep doing tasks that need to be completed in your life. In this whole process, you learn to become a happier person. You learn to *choose* happiness as a mindset. You now know it starts with you.

I've been discussing anger and resentment throughout *The Art of Forgiveness* and the *YIPPEE Method* chapters. These two emotions need to be overcome in order to live in peace and be free. Therefore, I'd like to further explore them in the next chapter. I'll be relaying the ways in which anger and resentment form, what's behind them, and how to resolve and rise above them. This is the crux of how you can gain empowerment from these feelings. Join me in Chapter 6 as I review these things.

To close this chapter, think back on all the stages of the *YIPPEE Method* we've discussed. If not yet completed, finish using the *Method* to work through the one resentment on which you chose to work. When you have completed this resentment from the *Process* stage, journal about your successes and difficulties. Include what you were/are feeling. Then work through each resentment you listed in the *Investigate* stage. Work on them one at a time to the end. This may take more than one sitting. Once your task is completed, come with me to more fully understand your anger, your resentment, so you can resolve them more deeply...

PART III

Becoming Whole

CHAPTER 6
Anger, Resentment, and Beyond

"Forgiveness is not an occasional act; it is a permanent attitude."
— Dr. Martin Luther King, Jr.

"Forgiveness washes away from the soul
The dust of everyday life."
— Dr. Jim Dincalci

Preparing for Peace

The anger and resentment under the violence occurring in the country and the world can and must be addressed and healed. This can be accomplished by examining the anger to heal what fuels it – the feelings and wounds underneath. When this exploration occurs, forgiveness happens. This is one way to perhaps make an impact on the gun violence. Wounds can be healed, thus, resolving the shooter's desire to hurt another. It is possible to do this, to get beyond anger and resentment, as my story in this book demonstrates. Furthermore, this is what the experts say. Dr. Jim Dincalci, university instructor, founder and CEO of The Forgiveness Foundation, and retired child and family therapist, tells us peace and joy can be achieved after feeling years of anger and resentment.

He says in his book, *How to Forgive When You Can't*, it is possible to heal a lifetime of anger, blame, resentment, grudges, and especially regret, guilt, and self-blame, so you can enjoy more peace and joy in your life. My experiences that evolved into peace and joy are perfect examples of what Dr. Dincalci writes are possible.

Another perspective is from Dr. Fred Luskin, Ph.D. counselor and health psychologist at Stanford University. He is the Director and Co-founder of The Stanford Forgiveness Project. This groundbreaking work uncovered many things about forgiveness, including the health benefits to one who forgives. In his book, *Forgive for Good*, he tells us it is absolutely possible to get from a place of emotional upset to one of peace by using forgiveness.

In *Overcoming Destructive Anger*, Dr. Bernard Golden, Ph.D. psychologist of forty years and the founder of Anger Management Education, tells us, "...your attitude and everything you've learned about anger are embedded in your brain's neural pathways." He goes on to add, "But neuroscientists say that people can reeducate their brains." He claims that if we cultivate new ways of reacting and thinking, we can grow fresh connections to new neurons. Doing this leads to new patterns in the brain, as well as new habits. Therefore, Dr. Golden validates my premise, as well as Dr. Dincalci's and Dr. Luskin's beliefs - angry and resentful people *can* grow beyond those emotions to gain peace. The ability to do so lies in the hands of the angry person and perhaps in the hands of each of us. Does it need to be our responsibility to take the initiative to learn new ways of managing anger and resentment, then making it available to those who need it?

During the early years of recovery and healing, I was forced to look at my anger without anything to numb it - this after thirty years of stuffing it. Well, actually, it came out sometimes when I was very drunk. And sometimes, at awkward times, I blew my stack. This mostly occurred in private with my husband. I also got angry with other people, though I didn't rant to their face. I complained and got angry in private.

Mostly, I turned my anger inward, attacking myself with words and thoughts about how inadequate I was – worthless and stupid. The negative things I could say about myself came from my lips or ran across my mind. This inner anger led to an inability to be empowered. In fact, it kept me a victim for many, many years, depressed and in despair.

At six or seven years sober, I kept praying to God to let me die. I was too afraid to commit suicide, was afraid I'd fail. It all worked out, obviously, and it was Spirit who gave me the gift of being able to recognize my purpose in life. I thought I had none, other than to be bearing the results of a difficult childhood.

There may be some of you who are reading this book and are sure you need to end it all. I understand. Yet, there is another way. You do have a purpose on this Earth. Rather than create a self-prison, rather than allow your feelings to extinguish a life you discovered earlier was a miracle, I invite you to use this book as a guide to set yourself free. I invite you to become able to identify your true feelings underneath the feelings of utter despair. It's a matter of taking one thing at a time, just one. Once you identify your feelings, you can then begin to heal them.

The Ultimate Tragedy of Anger and Resentment

In addition to the tragedy of creating a self-prison, or taking our own lives, we see with increasing frequency the tragedy of anger and resentment in mass shootings. In the November 11, 2018 San Francisco *Chronicle*, Jonathan J. Cooper and Michael Balsamo wrote about the anger of Ian David Long, the shooter at the bar in Thousand Oaks, California. They stated, "Dominique Colell, who coached girls' track and field at the high school where Long was a sprinter, remembers an angry young man who could be verbally and physically combative." They went on to say, "In one instance, Colell said Long used his fingers to mimic shooting her in the head..."

Despite being a teenager, Mr. Long displayed signs he was a danger to others, and quite possibly with a gun. How was he missed as a potential shooter? The Thousand Oaks shooting represents an ultimate tragedy that occurs when feelings beneath anger and resentment are not identified, acknowledged, and healed - even as a teen, especially as a teen.

Perhaps, when we see an angry person, we focus on avoiding him/her, rather than facilitating healing. This could be due to our aversion to absorbing the toxicity he/she exudes. Perhaps, it's the drained feeling we get when around an angry or resentful person, as the expressed emotions drag us down and tire us out. Certainly, it could be related to our fear of getting hurt, even shot. If my assessment of why we avoid angry people is correct, how do we as individuals – you and I – and society in general, allow ourselves to connect with them?

If there were to be a system or process whereby angry and resentful people were identified or self-identified, perhaps there could be a way to reach a potential shooter. He/she could be offered assistance with healing. If this happened, perhaps we would see a decrease in gun violence. Even if a shooter weren't reached, there would be more peace.

As I type, there is a mass shooting in New Zealand. These massacres are senseless and do nothing except to serve as a means for the shooter to express anger and resentment. They reveal their hate and hostility toward those who are different than they. It is not acceptable despite the fact that he/she may think it's okay to gun down groups of people he/she hates, all due to differences – differences in appearance, customs, beliefs, thoughts, and ideas. Is there a way we can, as a society, learn to embrace our differences, to make friends with them? It starts with individuals learning to appreciate each other.

I say all of this and, yet, shootings continue. I contend if a shooter's anger and resentment were identified and healed, these shootings could decrease in frequency. The lessening of feelings underlying the person's anger, such as hurt, shame, humiliation, and disappointment could occur and serve to prevent his/her fuse from lighting. It could prevent the aftermath of destructive anger. Imagine. If gaining peace and freedom from resentment could be possible for someone who is carrying wounds such that they'd shoot others, consider the effect the art of forgiveness might have on someone who does not consider violence as an option to resolve issues; it would be huge.

Dr. Golden makes a very important point I'd like to stress. He states if one gains greater self-awareness, it often leads to recognition of the anguish that provoked the anger in the first place. His statement reinforces the point I advocate. When we explore our behavior, thoughts, and feelings as I've suggested - in other words, develop greater self-awareness as Dr. Golden recommends - we learn what our feelings are under the anger. Then we can begin to heal.

The Behaviors of a Resentment

In his book, *Overcoming Destructive Anger*, Dr. Golden says, "We hold on to anger to avoid taking responsibility." Plus, "...anger can distract you from having to take responsibility for your decisions. It's often much easier to blame others for your suffering." The blaming that occurs across the country is amazing! Rather than spewing blame for another, I invite you to explore *your* behavior and let the blame go. You reap huge benefits when you look at your words and actions rather than blaming the other.

As Dr. Golden points out, many, many people hold their anger and resentment for years. Some never become willing or able to make the commitment necessary "...to define the structure and meaning of [their] life and to take the steps to live it." In my position as a senior caregiver, I observe elders who are not able or willing to look at their feelings over a long-term resentment, let alone express them. Instead, they continue to reference the event with bitterness. It saddens me they don't give themselves a chance to gain freedom from the prison they have created in their hearts.

How is one to get to the place beyond these feelings, beyond the anger and resentment? Dr. Golden recommends mindfulness, mindfulness meditation, self-compassion, and self-awareness. He suggests we practice these things to encourage the expression of healthy anger versus destructive anger.

Ms. Casarjian in *Houses of Healing* discusses a visualization that warrants mention. When you practice "seeing" another or yourself as a person who has a peaceful, loving, and wise nature, you start to look for and find these qualities in the person you resent. She recommends you begin to look for the peaceful, loving, and wise qualities in that person and then bring these feelings to your mind. Do this three times a day for thirty days. After that, you begin to see the other as a peaceful, loving, and wise being.

To do this, Ms. Casarjian believes you must have a vision of your adult Self, and know your Self is filled with peace, love, and wisdom. Consider becoming aware of others and yourself at this very level. After completing a self-appraisal, can you receive and accept this nature of your being - your peace, love, and wisdom? Can you identify these qualities in yourself? Are you able to receive praise graciously or do you push against the compliment? I invite you to write about what surfaces as you contemplate these questions.

Ms. Casarjian says by forgiving someone and "seeing" them, you begin to heal the habitual judgments you make. The same is true about your grown up Self. When you "see" your Self, when you are *aware* of your Self and receive it graciously, you begin to heal the separation you may be experiencing inside.

Dealing with Grievances

In *Forgive for Good,* Dr. Luskin spells out a way to get beyond anger and resentment. In it, he discusses grievances. He explores a way to consider what is behind these emotions.

He clarifies that a grievance forms when something we really wanted to happen did not materialize. Furthermore, Dr. Luskin goes on to state when we are faced with the unexpected disappointment, we are sometimes not equipped emotionally to handle these feelings. At this point, we develop a grievance, a resentment. On the other hand, when we cope and deal well with the experience, we avoid developing a grievance.

Additionally, Dr. Luskin explains, "A grievance emerges when two things coincide. The first is that something happens in our lives that we did not want to happen. Then, second, we deal with this problem by thinking about it too much..." He talks further about the way in which we start paying rent in our minds over the problem. He relays, when these things occur, we need to deal with the disappointment that arises. If we don't, we get angry and resentful.

I'd like to review the behaviors that indicate you have a grievance. There are three of them in which you engage, according to Dr. Luskin. When you're resenting, when you have a grievance, you are:

1. Taking the offense too personally,

2. Blaming the offender for how you feel, and
3. Telling your grievance story over and over again to whomever will listen.

These three behaviors present themselves again and again when we have a grievance, a resentment. Let's explore Dr. Luskin's further definition of the above points and the way to manage each...

Overly Reacting to an Offense

The first response you have when you experience a resentment is to react and take it too personally, as if the offender intended to hurt you. Yet, most of the time, another is thinking about himself/herself, not about you. He/she may likely be trying to deal with his/her *own* grievance story. That's another reason he/she is likely not thinking of you when you were offended. Dr. Luskin claims others are often more worried about getting something they don't have or keeping something they do have then they are in you.

The offender may hurt you in the same way he/she was hurt. This is done without consideration of you, as Dr. Sandra Wilson states in her book, *Hurt People Hurt People*. She claims people who hurt each other surround us. They hurt each other because of the "...seemingly inescapable pain in their own lives." One thing you learn from Dr. Wilson's book is people hurt others in the same ways they have been hurt. Knowing this can assist in your ability to forgive, thus, empowering yourself. By knowing all of this, you can make the choice to let go of taking the offense personally.

My offender told me disparaging words for years - words that followed me throughout my life. As soon as I realized he/she could have meant these words about himself/herself and not about me, this helped me to stop taking the offense personally. In fact, it was at this point I began to gain compassion for the offender. That, as you know, evolved into forgiveness. When you begin to cease taking the offense too personally, you feel the emotion of compassion, coupled with empathy. You are ready to look at the second point Dr. Luskin discusses in his book - playing the blame game.

Blaming Others

We blame others for our misfortunes. Dr. Luskin believes we do this in search of a reason why the calamity came to us in the first place. This is coupled with Dr. Golden's important point I mentioned earlier – blaming occurs as a means of avoiding responsibility. When I left my marriage and ran into the unrequited love wall, at first I blamed my husband. You see if his behavior had been kinder, more respectful, and less volatile, there would have been no need to leave. This was my story. I changed it once I was in the middle of my two-month drunk. At that time, I started blaming myself for the whole thing. I became engulfed by regret, remorse, and self-hate.

The fact is I created my own anguish because of the manner in which I left the marriage. I set myself up for the crash. I created angst for the dock mate, my husband, and myself. With my husband, there was no communication, no discussion before I dropped the bombshell that I was leaving our marriage. I can't even *imagine* what he was feeling at that time. Surely, I caused tremendous pain. I couldn't visualize or really comprehend the depth of the pain I likely caused until roughly three years ago. This was the same time period during which I began to identify deep understanding of my past behavior and how it affected, and might still affect, the other person.

You see, at the time I left the marriage, I was not adept at considering my feelings or behaviors. I didn't know how to do that. I only considered the blame and what my ex and others did to me, until I blamed myself. In these situations,

Dr. Luskin defines a choice you have. You can blame the offender *or* you can look at *your* role in the situation. *Your* role has to do with unenforceable rules you have imposed on another or yourself. These rules are arbitrary, often based on getting your own way. They are usually unrealistic and not achievable. Let's take a look at them...

When Expectations Are Resentments Waiting to Happen

Dr. Luskin refers to unenforceable rules that usually lead to resentment. Often, if you find you are resentful, you are exerting a rule, expecting more from others and/or yourself than they, or you, can give. This was the story of my life. In an effort to enforce my unrealistic rules that were not enforceable, I saw only negative responses to them, only "unwillingness" by others to adhere to my rules. Following them was difficult, however, as most were unspoken.

When I got angry at someone for breaking my silent rules, I missed finding the delightful positives in the situation, the lessons being learned, the possibilities emerging - the gratitudes! I didn't even know these things existed. All I knew was if someone didn't follow my rules, it was instant anger followed by resentment. I kept track of these and pulled them out during arguments.

In current day, I keep an eye on the signs I'm forming an unenforceable rule with unrealistic expectations. As soon as I find myself envisioning how things will look in a certain situation, I know there's a rule in the making. Instead, my ultimate goal is to let things happen as they will, let people be who they are, and accept it all as it is. I want to delight in seeing how things unfold.

Exploring Unenforceable Rules

I invite you to explore *your* unenforceable rules, the unrealistic expectations you place on others *and* yourself.

Make a list of them. Then, one rule at a time, consider the questions below. If you ask these, you can gain more control over the rules you place on others and yourself. The experts recommend you ask and answer:

1. From where did this rule originate?
2. Do I believe it to be truth?
3. Can I become willing to look deeply and with intention at my expectation?
4. Would that intention be to change my behavior?
5. Do I see it as a learning tool?
6. Is it humanly possible to adhere to my rule?

Let's look a bit more closely. We cannot expect others to follow the rules we have mandated - sometimes arbitrarily. I know someone who is a textbook example of a person with unenforceable rules. He/she has devised a host of rules for others to follow. Most are unrealistic and unattainable, based on antiquated equipment, activities, and beliefs. He/she is adamant people follow the rules and when they balk or simply don't adhere, he/she becomes irritated and builds a resentment. This extremely rigid behavior is very difficult to be around while trying to maintain peace. Even so, imagine the unhappiness the person may experience.

As an example of an unenforceable rule, let me share one unwritten rule of mine - an unenforceable one. It is the way in which I expect to be acknowledged by clerks at stores. For example, when they are busy with a customer that will take a while and I'm next in line, I expect them to at least let me know they realize I'm there. Mind you, I never *say* anything to make them aware of me. After all, their acknowledgment of me is merely being polite on their part. Isn't it part of their job? I expect an acknowledgment so I know I won't be forgotten due to the difficulty with the current customer. A nod is perfect. Any type of indication they see me is fine.

Once they acknowledge me, they go on uninterrupted with their current customer and I'm satisfied. When they don't do this after I've been there for several minutes, I get upset and clear my throat or cough as a means of getting them to notice and acknowledge me.

I want to believe the clerk will let me know he/she sees me. It's clearly a rule I cannot enforce. Perhaps, he/she believes it would be rude to interrupt the customer being served in the moment, yet, I'm not asking they be interrupted. At any rate, as I explored why I tend to get upset when the clerks don't acknowledge me, I discovered an old wound. It was the wound of not receiving acknowledgment for years. From that experience, I got the message I wasn't being seen, wasn't valued or wanted.

This wound of mine festered and grew into the feeling I had no worth, no value. Apparently, this rears its ugliness when the clerks don't acknowledge me. It points out there is more healing required of me, more self-worth I need to establish. Here again I have a choice. There's *always* a choice. I can choose to take this information and attempt to improve upon my feelings of worthiness, or I can continue to act based on a sense of unworthiness, in other words, feelings of worthlessness. I choose worthiness. I choose it because it is the truth of who I am. It's the truth of who *you* are, too. It's the truth of who we *all* are.

In the situation I just described about the clerk, the wisdom and nugget are that I am now aware of this behavior and can be alert for it. I don't have to get the clerk to acknowledge me anymore. Instead, I can wait patiently for my turn. I can politely speak up if he/she begins to wait on someone behind me in line. (That's the fear, of course - someone may take my turn in line, may make me invisible.) Best of all, I can further my feelings of worthiness. That's the biggest nugget. For these things, I am grateful.

This level of scrutiny is very valuable for you in your healing journey. In my example about the clerk, I am *choosing* to seek the positive in this situation, rather than beat up, chide, or denigrate myself in any way. I have learned to look with curiosity, not shame. When I look at my behavior from a situation in which I tried to exert an unenforceable and unrealistic rule, I initially experience a little embarrassment. That goes away once I become curious, as I can see the wisdom and golden nugget I'm learning. Where in *your* life can you apply this process of exploration? Identify one example of an unenforceable rule you place on another. Write it down. Consider whether this is unrealistic or unreachable. Write about what you discover.

Dr. Dincalci tells us, often someone else in your life set your rules and you are merely mirroring what that person did or said. You may not believe in their values so the rules aren't a reflection of you. Perhaps, you're exerting the rules of people you don't necessarily like or respect. You may wish to portray your own values and beliefs. Perhaps, you hold others to the standard of perfection. Perfect is not achievable. There is no such thing. That's because we are, ultimately, flawed humans, unable to produce perfection from the non-perfect. Given these things, it's a good time to reassess where those unenforceable rules came from and choose whether you'll continue to "enforce" them, knowing they are futile and lead to resentment. It is also a good time to assess the expectations your rules generate.

As you look at the unenforceable rule you identified from the exercise above, consider whether you are exerting your rule on the person you currently resent. Once you explore this, I invite you to consider what he/she might do to meet your rule. Is the rule reasonable? Could you achieve it if the roles were reversed? If you can't, consider changing your rules. Repeat this exercise, this time looking at the rules you place on yourself. Ask the same questions...

Singing the Song of a Hero

Let's examine the third thing Dr. Luskin claims you do when you have a resentment, which is to tell a tale of woe, a grievance story. You tell it over and over and over again to whomever will listen. There is a distinction between telling a grievance story and telling another of a situation with which you are angry or upset. When you repeatedly tell your tale of woe to the same people, you are probably entrenched in your story. When you do this at the same time you are blaming the other, not taking steps to move forward in your life, these are signs it's a grievance story.

On the other hand, to share with someone the difficulty you encountered is a helpful and healthful thing to do. As relayed in the *YIPPEE Method*, speaking with another about feelings you uncover is crucial. The difference is, in a healthy situation, you relay it once or twice to a trusted person. Then you move forward in your life and become able to sing the song of a hero rather than remain a victim.

"How do I do that?" you may ask. "How do I sing the song of a hero?" According to Dr. Luskin, ask and answer these three powerful questions about your anger and resentment, your grievance:

1. What is the lesson(s) I learned from this experience?
2. What positive thing(s) came about because of the situation?
3. What can I be grateful for?

When you ask and answer these questions, you become inspired and *inspiring*. Not only does it offer inspiration to you and others, it actually gives permission to others to sing their *own* song of a hero instead telling a tale of woe. This is a feeling you want to experience!

The above questions and thought processes of Dr. Luskin's were instrumental in allowing me to transcend my grief over the unrequited love. I rose above the grief permanently. The questions posed are especially valuable in dissolving resentment; yet, they work on grief as well. I invite you to apply them to a current grievance you carry. Once you do this, notice how your attitude shifts. Write about the feelings once they change. If you did not experience a difference in mindset, write your thoughts explaining why you think you didn't. Repeat the questions. If needed, keep doing this until you feel grateful for the event or person you resent.

This wraps up the exploration of anger and resentment. As you leave this chapter, tuck away the golden nuggets from the experts. Come back here for reference when needed. As an endorsement, I've experienced everything these masters say about the causes of anger and resentment and how to manage them. It's all truth. Turn the page to examine what you receive when you can get beyond your anger, your resentment, and live a promise of peace...

CHAPTER 7

Living a Promise of Peace

"Life isn't about waiting for the storm to pass.
It's about learning how to dance in the rain."
— Vivian Greene

Making the Journey

When I visited Yosemite National Park, I was two years sober and traveling in the van. On that day I was feeling good about things. After driving, hiking, and being awed by the spectacular sights, I went to the gift shop. While wandering through, I noticed a book by Oriah Mountain Dreamer. It was titled after the poem it contained - *The Invitation*. The start of the poem was printed on the cover jacket in a beautiful font. There was a feather alongside the prose. I felt a sudden visual connection, followed closely by a visceral connection to the words and emotions so eloquently scribed. On the inner front of the jacket was the following statement with which I deeply resonated:

> *"The Invitation* is a declaration of intent, a map into the longing of the soul, the desire to live passionately, face-to-face with ourselves and skin-to-skin with the world around us."

The expression in these words of living closely and passionately with the world and myself spoke volumes to me. I *longed* to live passionately, to connect with others and myself at that level! I became excited and bought the book. From it, I gained a deep longing to live fully, taking in each moment. This book, more than any other, kept me sober when I was the most down, devastated, and wanted to drink. It brought me great solace.

It was not until fifteen years sober, three years ago, I *truly* began living the life Ms. Mountain Dreamer portrays is available and possible for us – for each of us. For me, for you. Now, as I live in that space, I look back with great fondness at the way in which *The Invitation* affected the course of my life's travels. I bring up the story of buying this book to let you know what she describes is reality in my life today. It can be reality in your life as well. There are only accolades I can offer for the life so dear to me now. I am truly living passionately from my soul. This affects me and the world around me. Now you, too, have the tools, knowledge, and heart-space to live from your soul, in touch with yourself and those around you.

That's not to say there is no work to be done, for there is. Ms. Mountain Dreamer said it well when she claimed, "Feeling the pull of the heart or the quickening of the blood that urges movement forward, is not the same thing as actually making the journey." Sometimes moving forward is difficult. However, like it did for me, life can become dear for you, too. It takes the commitment to stick with it, even if criticized or ridiculed by a spouse, friend, or parent. Stick with it even if you can't see where the journey is leading, even if you want to quit – *especially* when you want to quit. Know others have been where you are now and there is support from them during difficult times. Recall the meanings of HOPE. Remember to write in your journal to process your feelings. As always, I invite and encourage you to use your "other" hand. The rewards are amazing!

To make the journey, you develop willingness to do the work to the best of your abilities. On the other end of the spectrum, you'll need willingness to receive the rewards, the awe and wonder that come to you, the sense of calm and serenity.

Along the way, it helps to develop the skills to persevere and yearn. Discover a way to *yearn* for peace and freedom from your anger, grievance, and stress. Develop and offer compassion, kindness, and love to yourself and others during the course of your journey and theirs.

By reading how I've reached this level and depth of self-assessment, you may form the conclusion you are able to get to the same level and depth as soon as you've read this book. That's awesome; I applaud you and your desire! In case you want to push them, though, I invite you to let your feelings bubble naturally to the surface on their own accord without forcing or rushing them.

If you are reading and observing my journey, perhaps you are thinking you "should" be able to do the same thing or things tomorrow that I speak of in the book. This is a wonderful intention and vision to hold in your heart, your soul! Be sure to keep that in your being. You may wish to re-assess this goal, though, after you've worked through the *Investigate* stage of the *YIPPEE Method*. It could take longer than you thought it might, or that it "should." There's that shaming "should" again... Avoid getting trapped by the "shoulds."

The point I'm trying to make is what Ms. Mountain Dreamer so gracefully explains. She states when you get in touch with your joy and sorrow, layer-upon-layer of feelings are exposed. She claims, "If you take the journey, real change is possible and inevitable, and, from the present vantage point, completely unpredictable." Realize it is impossible to know what will come up for you or the other person; be prepared for any feelings or responses that arise.

Based on this bit of wisdom, I invite you to establish realistic goals and desires. By doing so, you avoid disappointment or discouragement that the feelings arising from yourself or another are not as anticipated or desired. And yes, by you knowing various bits of information I've been sharing, you can move forward more quickly than I moved. Mostly, your success depends upon the desire to be at peace, soaring free, and your willingness level.

According to Dr. Dincalci, it also takes moving beyond fear. I mentioned this earlier; it bears repeating. He claims, "Feelings might resurface as you start looking at your upsets and you might not want to continue. This is just a smoke screen put up by fear. In nature, the hunted will often turn to fight. When monstrous situations from the past haunt you mercilessly, attack is sometimes the best defense. If you are committed to slaying your demons and facing them head on, they will lose their power to frighten or harm you." I invite you to stick with your self-exploration, despite feelings that arise and haunt you. By doing this, you prompt the healing process to begin. Doing so will allow you to get beyond fear. Even as you do this, heed Dr. Luskin's warning to prevent getting attached to being down or feeling angry.

Ms. Mountain Dreamer enlightens us in *The Invitation* when she relays, "...no part of the journey is wasted." Know and realize each experience, each effort, each time it doesn't go according to plans or wishes, has a place in the scheme of your growth and healing. Someday, the experience will prove valuable. One day you will know peace and joy from what occurred. You will even understand the purpose of this hurtful and stressful event. After adopting the belief there are no mistakes in the world of Spirit, you can deepen your trust in and relationship with that force.

Positive Affirmations

Remember my unhealed need to be acknowledged by store clerks? After I became aware of the underlying wound and the feelings of worthlessness generated from that wound, I worked to resolve it. Every time it came up, I directed my awareness to the fact that I was *worthy* of attention. I reinforced in my mind and heart that I was a worthy being, filled with love and kindness for others. I held love and kindness for myself.

Certainly, the clerk's lack of acknowledgment was not a reflection of my value. He/she was merely focusing on the job. Ah, sanity prevailed. From this experience, I have gained the skill of patience. Along with it comes the realization and belief that I *am* a valuable and valued woman! This leads me to feel empowered, as I am in control of the stressors in my life.

Dr. Dincalci might agree what I described were positive affirmations when I talked to myself and redirected my energy to my worthiness. These affirming positive statements about yourself said throughout the day are intended to produce a mind shift. As he writes in his book, *How to Forgive When You Can't,* Dr. Dincalci believes these positive statements work to make that shift because a positive emotional intention is established.

Dr. Golden in *Overcoming Destructive Anger* defines an exercise in which you become acutely aware of a simple act. In his example, it is eating a raisin. In that act, you notice every detail of the experience. This primes you for mindfulness meditation. The technique allows you to see your thoughts go by in your mind without judgment or contemplation. Once practiced, Dr. Golden claims it gets easier to observe yourself and your thoughts without judgment. You are merely a witness to your mind's activity. Through practice, you can achieve a state whereby you do not react when confronted with anger. Rather, you "merely observe."

There are many techniques the experts I've mentioned here recommend. To get more detail, I invite you to read each one's book. I've read each that is listed in the *References* section on pages 132 and 133. They all contain excellent material, golden nugget after golden nugget, and tons of wisdom.

A Promise of Peace

I want to recognize you again for your time with and attention to this work we have explored together. I commend your efforts to manage your anger and resentment, and to heal! It's not easy to do what we've been discussing. The fact that you're willing to make changes is marvelous! I hold great gratitude for you! Now give yourself kudos, a pat on the back, and a "way to go" for taking the time to read this book and develop the attitude necessary for healing to occur. Remember: You're a piece of art in the making, evolving over time. Be patient. Perhaps, your art piece reveals buds on the stem of a plant. This means you are about to blossom...

It is my hope that in reading and working through this book, you have gleaned ways you can "be" in your life such that you have more peace, happiness, and joy. It is also my hope you have come to forgive your offender(s) and yourself through the use of the *YIPPEE Method*. You deserve recognition and support for your work, your healing activity. It is my closing desire that this book has carried you from an angry and resentful space to one filled with peace and freedom. Further, it is my desire to have reached you if you are angry or resentful with a desire to shoot someone. My hope is you no longer feel this way.

It's time to critique the effectiveness of the art of forgiveness and the *YIPPEE Method*. I invite you to step back and view what you have created. What have you gained that was not present when you started on this book's journey? What are three things you can take away to use in your life today?

Once you forgive, you'll begin to feel a host of feelings such as peace, joy, happiness, worthiness, calmness, and the list goes on. From these changes, you will notice more harmony in your life when you relate to others. Your personal relationships, including the one with yourself, improve vastly. You experience a physical lightness with an increased level of energy. From following the *YIPPEE Method,* your confidence and esteem grow. These are some of the benefits of working through the art of forgiveness.

Hopefully, you have gone beyond your sorrow and confusion to a place of peace and joy. Ms. Mountain Dreamer encourages you to touch the difficult places within when she states, "If we refuse to touch the places of sorrow or confusion within ourselves or others, we cannot cultivate the ability to be completely present in our moments of joy and ecstasy." Perhaps, as it was for me, you can discover that the depth of your sorrow allows the deep, deep peace and joy you will treasure. It is my hope you have become able to defeat the voices of doubt, lack of confidence and esteem, as well as self-deprecation. When you cultivate your ability to live with joy and ecstasy, you unearth confidence and esteem.

May you use this book as a vehicle to continue your journey while you deepen the levels of peace and freedom from your trials and difficulties. Although I tried above, it is difficult to sufficiently put into words the feelings available to you when you forgive, when you allow gratitude and love into your life. There are words such as peace, joy, love, and contentment. Yet, there are really no words to express the *depth* of the joy, the *depth* of your peace and calm, the *breadth* of your love. There is simply and quietly a promise of peace. This promise includes the ability to practice kindness, love, respect, tolerance, and patience, all while you practice compassion, gratitude, and forgiveness – for others *and* yourself. Through forgiveness, may you experience a promise of peace in your life.

Promise of Peace

"When you practice the principles of love
For yourself and others,
The gates of your heart melt into the glow of dusk
And peace rises to greet you."

Carolyn CJ Jones
Photo/verse duet from the book,
Opening the Gates of the Heart: A Journey of Healing

Blessings, cj

References

Introduction
- The Dalai Lama, http://iamfearless.com.

Chapter 1
- Dr. Fred Luskin, *Forgive for Good: A PROVEN Prescription for Health and Happiness*, HarperOne, an imprint of HarperCollins Publishing, 2002. pg. 3, 4, 7
- Ms. Mary Beth Sammons and Ms. Nina Lesowitz, *Living Life As a Thank You: The Transformative Power of Daily Gratitude*, Bristol Park, 2015. pg. 4
- Ms. Robin Casarjian, *Houses of Healing: A Prisoner's Guide to Inner Power and Freedom*, The Lionheart Foundation, 2007. pg. 4, 5, 13,14
- Dr. Jim Dincalci, *How to Forgive When You Can't: The Breakthrough Guide to Free Your Heart and Mind*, Ruah Press Edition, 2018. pg. 5
- Jeff Rose, *Good Financial Cents*, http://goodfinancialcents.com/blog, 2018. pg. 10
- *Healthpsych* magazine, http://healthypsych.com/psychology-tools-what-is-anger-a-secondary-emotion, 2018 pg. 12

Chapter 2
- Ms. Maura McCarley Torkildson, *Tackling Trauma*, http://quietwriting.com/tackling-trauma, 2019. pg. 24
- Dr. Fred Luskin, *Forgive for Good: A PROVEN Prescription for Health and Happiness*, HarperOne, an imprint of HarperCollins Publishing, 2002. pg. 28

Chapter 3

- Ms. Robin Casarjian, *Houses of Healing: A Prisoner's Guide to Inner Power and Freedom,* The Lionheart Foundation, 2007.pg. 33
- National Institute for the Clinical Application of Behavioral Medicine, http://NICABM.org 2017. pg. 34

Chapter 4

- Dr. Jim Dincalci, *How to Forgive When You Can't: The Breakthrough Guide to Free Your Heart and Mind,* Ruah Press Edition, 2018. pg. 53
- Dr. Sandra Wilson, *Hurt People Hurt People: Hope and Healing for Yourself and Your Relationships,* Discovery House, 2015. pg. 55

Chapter 5

- Ms. Robin Casarjian, *Houses of Healing: A Prisoner's Guide to Inner Power and Freedom,* The Lionheart Foundation, 2007. pg. 63, 71, 72, 75
- Dr. Fred Luskin, *Forgive for Good: A PROVEN Prescription for Health and Happiness,* HarperOne, an imprint of HarperCollins Publishing, 2002. pg. 64, 68, 74, 75
- Dr. Jim Dincalci, *How to Forgive When You Can't: The Breakthrough Guide to Free Your Heart and Mind,* Ruah Press Edition, 2018. pg. 75

Chapter 6

- Dr. Jim Dincalci, *How to Forgive When You Can't: The Breakthrough Guide to Free Your Heart and Mind,* Ruah Press Edition, 2018. pg. 82, 95
- Dr. Bernard Golden, *Overcoming Destructive Anger: Strategies That Work,* John Hopkins University Press, 2016. pg. 83, 86, 87, 90

- Dr. Fred Luskin, *Forgive for Good: A PROVEN Prescription for Health and Happiness*, HarperOne, an imprint of HarperCollins Publishing, 2002. pg. 83, 88, 89, 90, 91, 92, 96
- *San Francisco Chronicle*, Jonathan J, Cooper and Michael Balsamo, November 11, 2018. pg. 84
- Ms. Robin Casarjian, *Houses of Healing: A Prisoner's Guide to Inner Power and Freedom*, The Lionheart Foundation, 2007. pg. 87
- Dr. Sandra Wilson, *Hurt People Hurt People: Hope and Healing for Yourself and Your Relationships*, Discovery House, 2015. pg. 89

Chapter 7

- Ms. Oriah Mountain Dreamer, *The Invitation*, HarperCollins and HarperSan Francisco, trademarks of HarperCollins Publishers, Inc., 1999. pg. 98, 99, 100, 101, 104
- Dr. Jim Dincalci, *How to Forgive When You Can't: The Breakthrough Guide to Free Your Heart and Mind*, Ruah Press Edition, 2018. pg. 101, 102
- Dr. Bernard Golden, *Overcoming Destructive Anger: Strategies That Work*, John Hopkins University Press, 2016. pg. 102

About the Author

Born in a suburb of Philadelphia, Carolyn Jones was raised near Columbus, Ohio. Over the years, she slowly migrated to the West coast, where she currently lives in the San Francisco Bay Area. The move west began after she graduated from Kent State University School of Nursing in 1974 and moved to Colorado. There she worked as a nurse in various capacities. It was her love of sailing and boats that lured Carolyn to the coast. Once living in California, she and her husband lived on their boat for three years, at which time the marriage fell apart. Nine months later, Carolyn sought sobriety. It was at that time she retired from nursing.

Carolyn became an entrepreneur several years later. While researching to determine if she could be "found" by people searching for her, she looked herself up on Google. Up popped twenty-five pages and more of Carolyn Jones the actress. There was no way she could compete with this. The solution was to create a middle name. Even though she was not given one at birth, and because she did not take her husband's last name for professional reasons, Carolyn knew she had to use the nickname given to her by her high school friend. That nickname, CJ, became part of her official name as well as the name of her business. Most people believe it to be the initials for Carolyn Jones; they are incorrect. You see in high school, CJ was a lead in the musical *Carousel.* It was a ham part and she played it up. As a result, her friend named her the original Cracker Jack. That's what CJ stands for! And *this* is how CJ came to be as an integral part of her name and the creation of Carolyn CJ Jones. For more information about CJ, including other books, programs and services, visit www.carolyncjjones.com.

Also by Carolyn CJ Jones

Author | Speaker | Coach

The creation of *Opening the Gates of the Heart: A Journey of Healing* is a tribute to the resiliency and beauty of the human spirit. It enhances your journey to more joy, or guides you through a place of woundedness to peace and freedom. It is the recipient of the silver medal for world peace in the 2018 Living Now Evergreen Book Awards.

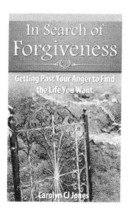

The ebook, *In Search of Forgiveness: Getting Past Your Anger to Find the Life You Want,* guides you through a method that brings you to a place of forgiveness. Along the way, you begin to experience more peace, joy, and finally, empowerment.

Made in the USA
Columbia, SC
22 September 2019